BFI FILM CLASS
. . . .
Rob White
S E R I E S   E D I T O R
Colin MacCabe and David Meeker
S E R I E S   C O N S U L T A N T S

Cinema is a fragile medium. Many of the great classic films of the past now exist, if at all, in damaged or incomplete prints. Concerned about the deterioration in the physical state of our film heritage, the National Film and Television Archive, a Division of the British Film Institute, has compiled a list of 360 key films in the history of the cinema. The long-term goal of the Archive is to build a collection of perfect showprints of these films, which will then be screened regularly at the Museum of the Moving Image in London in a year-round repertory.

BFI Film Classics is a series of books commissioned to stand alongside these titles. Authors, including film critics and scholars, film-makers, novelists, historians and those distinguished in the arts, have been invited to write on a film of their choice, drawn from the Archive's list. Each volume presents the author's own insights into the chosen film, together with a brief production history and detailed credits, notes and bibliography. The numerous illustrations have been specially made from the Archive's own prints.

With new titles published each year, the BFI Film Classics series is a unique, authoritative and highly readable guide to the great films of world cinema.

Could scarcely be improved upon ... informative, intelligent, jargon-free companions.
The Observer

Cannily but elegantly packaged BFI Classics will make for a neat addition to the most discerning shelves.
New Statesman & Society

Alphonse makes his fateful call to Doctor Nelson

**BFI FILM
CLASSICS**

LA NUIT AMÉRICAINE

....

Roger Crittenden

bfi Publishing

To Ed Buscombe for the opportunity …
it has meant more than can be imagined

First published in 1998 by the
BRITISH FILM INSTITUTE
21 Stephen Street, London W1P 2LN

The British Film Institute
is the UK national agency with
responsibility for encouraging the arts
of film and television and
conserving them in the national interest.

British Library Cataloguing-in-Publication Data
A catalogue record for this book is available from the British Library

ISBN 0–85170–672–X

Series design by
Andrew Barron & Collis Clements Associates

Typesetting by
D R Bungay Associates, Burghfield, Berks.

Printed in Great Britain by Norwich Colour Print

CONTENTS

The Dream Factory in its prosaic surroundings: the Victorine Studios on the outskirts of Nice

ACKNOWLEDGMENTS

. . . .

Les Films du Carrosse, Truffaut's production company, moved to its present premises in 1965, in rue Robert-Estienne just off the Champs-Elysées. At the end of this small cul-de-sac is a kindergarten, and the sound of children's voices swells to meet you as you approach. Truffaut had a special affinity to children and his spirit seems present in that sound.

His spirit is still present in those offices where his archive can be consulted by all those with a genuine interest in him and his films. For this we have to thank Madeleine Morgenstern, his former wife, who still runs the company, and Monique Holveck, her assistant, who was part of the Carrosse team for many years when Truffaut was alive. Their generosity and helpfulness is clearly at one with the kind of support François Truffaut was in the habit of giving to his fellow film-makers throughout his life.

The crew of the film have been very generous to me with their time, especially Suzanne Schiffman, Yann Dedet, Martine Barraqué, Pierre-William Glenn and Damien Lanfranchi.

It has also been invaluable to talk to members of the cast of the film, notably Nathalie Baye, Jacqueline Bisset and Nike Arrighi (Borghese). I am also grateful to Kika Markham (*Les Deux anglaises et le continent*) and Jo Blatchley (*L'Histoire d'Adèle H*) for sharing their memories of Truffaut with me.

More than a dozen years after his death the Truffaut 'family' retains that special quality they shared when working together on his films; a quality celebrated in *La Nuit américaine*.

Finally I wish to thank my dear friend Madame Arlette Kendall for her help in deciphering handwritten French texts.

The stills in the book are frame stills, taken from the BFI's print of the film, or production stills selected from the BFI Stills, Posters and Designs collection. Photographers: pp. 15 & 18, Raymond Cauchetier; pp. 47, 62 & 77, Pierre Zucca.

BAZIN'S MAYONNAISE

· ·

In the preface to his book *Les Films de ma vie* Truffaut wrote:

> When I was twenty I reproached André Bazin for considering films like mayonnaises that take or don't take … but I am sure we have all ended up adopting Bazin's mayonnaise theory because the practise of cinema has taught us a certain number of things:
>
> It demands as much effort to make a bad film as a good one;
>
> Our most sincere film can look like a practical joke;
>
> The one we do most casually may end up going around the world;
>
> An idiotic but energetic film can be better cinema than an intelligent but flabby film;
>
> The result is rarely proportionate to the effort put into it.[1]

La Nuit américaine (1973) is not 'a bad film' but 'Je vous présente Paméla', the film within the film, has no pretensions to quality. It is clear that the effort involved in making it is disproportionate to its worth.

Truffaut made the deliberate choice of containing *La Nuit américaine* within the shooting period of *Pamela*. The film opens on the set of a Parisian square. The camera follows a young man, played by Jean-Pierre Léaud, as he traverses the crowded square to the point where he slaps the face of an older man played by Jean-Pierre Aumont. A voice yells 'coupé' (cut) and immediately the crew are revealed, as preparations are made for a second take.

We learn that Aumont and Léaud are playing father and son in a melodrama in which the father runs off with the son's new wife. The mother, Séverine, played by Valentina Cortesa, is an ageing Hollywood star of European origin with a drink problem, and the former lover of Aumont. Jacqueline Bisset plays the young wife and represents a Hollywood star of the current generation. She is recovering from a nervous breakdown and has married a doctor. The producer is only too aware that she is an insurance risk.

Léaud has got his girlfriend Liliane (Dani) a job as a trainee script-girl on the film but is soon jealous of her flirtation with the stills man (Pierre Zucca). This mélange is overseen by Truffaut himself as the director, Ferrand, supported by his faithful script-girl, Joëlle, played by Nathalie Baye in her first substantial screen appearance.

As the film unfolds we are made aware of the dramas behind the scenes both with the cast and with the crew. In the funniest scene in the film Cortesa, the worse for drink, cannot remember her lines and is unable to exit through the door, consistently opening a cupboard instead.

Not surprisingly, the director is having nightmares and soon feels that just getting to the end of the shoot will be an achievement. Several performers refuse to act: from a pregnant 'secretary' who has not agreed to be seen in a swimming costume, to a recalcitrant cat which refuses to lap milk on cue, to Léaud when deserted by his girlfriend, and Bisset who, having comforted Léaud is betrayed by him to her husband.

It takes the death of the character played by Aumont in a car accident to rally the cast and crew for a final effort and the film is finished successfully. When asked by a television crew at the end of the shoot how it has gone, the props man insists that everything has been wonderful.

After the release of *La Nuit américaine* Truffaut defended the film within the film claiming a nostalgia for films that are not afraid to tell a story and that have no qualms about being melodramtic. Indeed he also said that if anything 'profound' is in the film he preferred to think it had got there in spite of him.

The only hope which sustains those of us who become addicted to working in cinema is that after each film ends there will be another one that we can be a part of. The enjoyment of the finished product has little to do with its quality and more to do with the way it reminds us of the journey we took with our colleagues during its making.

I remember attending a cast and crew screening of Ken Russell's *Women in Love*. I had worked with Ken a number of times and knew several of the crew. After the show I said how much I had enjoyed the film but I also made one or two criticisms to those around me in the preview theatre. Their resentment was palpable.

I had forgotten that the contributors to a film invariably want to retain that sense of camaraderie that has kept them going for several months. Any 'outsider', however friendly, should not venture to question the value of the blood, sweat and tears that they have shed, even if in their hearts they might agree with the criticisms. With any luck the worst disillusionment felt after a film has been finished can be buried in the enthusiasm associated with the next.

It was certainly of paramount concern to Truffaut that his film would convey the closeness and temporary intimacy which characterise the most felicitous productions. This was no easy task when you take into account the ingredients he was using to make his mayonnaise: established actors from three different countries; ingénues from acting school, theatre, or minor roles; actors playing technicians; technicians playing themselves; even amateurs – who happened to live nearby or were visiting friends on the set – all directed by the director playing himself. 'If this works,' he said afterwards, 'then I am happy'.

The complexity of this situation is epitomised by the moment when the actress playing the make-up girl becomes an actress playing an actress and confuses another actress who is used to make-up girls being make-up girls and actresses being actresses!

In truth Truffaut conveyed the impression of a marvellously close-knit family on the screen. More than once in his career Truffaut expressed his admiration, even envy, of Ingmar Bergman's 'family'. In his memoires he wrote: 'The ideal is the little troupe of Bergman. Myself, I adore to find the same actors in the films of Bergman, I find that tremendous. … He is like the director of a theatre troupe.'[2]

It was partly because of his theatre work that Bergman managed such intimacy. Truffaut created something similar by founding Les Films du Carrosse. That it should be represented in his mind as analogous to the family, is a poignant reminder that his own childhood family had been anything but close or warm. On the other hand, despite the fact that his marriage to Madeleine Morgenstern lasted only a few short years, his attachment to her and their two daughters never wavered: they were by his bedside when he died.

But Bergman created a particular body of work with his 'family'. Almost all his films are intense chamber pieces; even *Fanny and Alexander*, his masterpiece, is only epic in length, not in scale or treatment. Nor are Bergman's films the kind of entertainment that is commercially orientated. If they relate at all to Truffaut's work it is to *Les Deux anglaises et le continent* (1971) or *La Chambre verte* (1978).

Ironically, though these two films were close to Truffaut's heart, they were not among his commercial successes. In the end there was too much tension between the films he wanted to make and his desire to reach the widest possible audience for him to be able to create a consistently personal and intense body of work.

The most revealing of Truffaut's comments about cinematic mayonnaise is: 'An idiotic but energetic film can be better cinema than an intelligent but flabby film', because it shows his overriding concern for what he called 'dynamic' films. Of course he would have preferred to make intelligent films that were energetic, but it is interesting that he says 'better cinema' rather than more successful. This makes his definition of good cinema dependent on energy rather than intelligence.

With *La Nuit américaine* he need not have worried, but worry he did, as always. In a letter to Jean Hugo in April 1973 he wrote that he had just completed a particularly difficult film. Perhaps it was caution that made him decide to offer the film for the opening at Cannes rather than enter it in competition, but I prefer to believe it was an instinctive decision, made in the knowledge that such a celebration of cinema could not fail to please in that context.

That opening night in Cannes, 14 May 1973, was perhaps Truffaut's apotheosis. Anyone who has seen the footage of his triumphal ascendance of the staircase of the Grand Palais, arm in arm with four of his leading actresses, cannot fail to agree that Truffaut had finally brought together in public his two loves – cinema and women in a public display worthy of a Middle Eastern potentate.

The triumph was to continue, reaching its zenith in Hollywood where Truffaut received the Oscar for Best Foreign Film. In his acceptance speech to the assembled masses of the cinema industry, he modestly said it was their award as the film was a celebration of cinema. But if they didn't mind, he added, he would look after it for them. Truffaut followed the film around the US, confident, once the New York Critics Circle had showered him with accolades (Best Picture, Best Director and Best Supporting Actress for Valentina Cortesa), that the film was a success.

The story back home was, however, rather different; both publicly and privately. When released in Paris the critics were full of praise, forgetting the failure of Truffaut's two previous films: *Les Deux anglaises et le Continent* (1971) and *Une belle fille comme moi* (1972). Although there were 300,000 admissions in Paris, the response in the provinces was only lukewarm.

Industry pundits felt that the man in the street imagined it to be either a documentary on the cinema or an overtly intellectual film. The idea of the film within the film was a conceit which, it was felt would put many people off. The publicity had subsequently to drop all mention of 'story of a shoot'. Even the title was a problem and the preferred approach to publicity was summed up by 'A Franco–Hollywood night of love between Jean-Pierre Léaud and Jacqueline Bisset'.

Truffaut was conscious that he was treading a delicate line with the film, and could imagine offending both his colleagues in the business with the banal nature of 'Je vous présente Pamela', and the lay audience on account of the relative complexity of the narrative form. And indeed many film people were disappointed by the image he had conveyed of the inside story of a shoot, not least his old comrade-in-arms, Jean-Luc Godard.

Godard and Truffaut had not been close for some time. By 1968 Truffaut felt that they had very little in common. From his point of view, however, the bond forged between them at *Cahiers du cinéma* meant that it was a matter of trust not to fall out publicly. By 1973 Godard's career had stalled with his failure to secure the necessary 'avance sur receipts' for his next project.

Having seen *La Nuit américaine* in May 1973 Godard vented his spleen in a vituperative letter to Truffaut. In it he said:

> Yesterday I saw *La Nuit américaine*. Probably no one else will call you a liar, so I will. … You say: films are trains that pass in the night, but who takes the train, in what class, and who is driving it with an 'informer' from the management standing at his side? … Liar because the shot of you and Jacqueline Bisset the other evening at Chez Francis is not in your film, and one can't help wondering why the director is the only one who doesn't screw in *La Nuit américaine*.[3]

With references to other film-makers he despises, Godard goes on to ascribe his problems financing his film to Truffaut and those like him who make expensive films, and he requests that Truffaut finance his new film.

Truffaut's lengthy response seems to have been provoked more by a letter Godard sent to Jean-Pierre Léaud via Truffaut – which Truffaut returned rather than pass on – than by any personal bitterness towards Godard. Truffaut was convinced that Godard had treated his protégé badly on *Masculin–Féminin*. But he had not intervened, despite knowing that Godard had bad-mouthed him during that shoot. Perhaps the most relevant paragraph in Truffaut's reply is when he says:

I don't give a shit what you think of *La Nuit américaine*, what I find deplorable on your part is the fact that even now, you continue to go and see such films, films whose subject matter you know in advance will not correspond to either your conception of the cinema or your conception of life.[4]

Truffaut piles up the evidence both of Godard's bad behaviour and of Truffaut's loyalty to him over the years. He notes poignantly that:

In Rome, I quarrelled with Moravia because he suggested that I film *Le Mépris*; I had gone there with Jeanne [Moreau] to present *Jules et Jim*; your latest film wasn't doing too well and Moravia was hoping to change horses in mid-stream.[5]

He refers here to the Alberto Moravia story about a film being made at Cinecittà, the studios in Rome. Godard filmed it in 1963. If Truffaut had made this film would he later have wanted to make *La Nuit américaine*? The world of cynicism and alienation conveyed in *Le Mépris*, certainly suited Godard more than Truffaut, so it was no real sacrifice for him to reject the solicitation of Moravia. We must, however, accept his honest anger at the idea that he would even consider usurping the other director's place.

It is of interest to note that in 1996 it was *Le Mépris* and not *La Nuit américaine* that was re-issued in Britain. There may be reasons for this more associated with distribution rights than with contemporary taste, but I wonder whether today's audiences prefer the hard edge of the Godard film to Truffaut's brand of humanism.

Perhaps Truffaut's time has yet to come again. In the ten years that he had left of life and film-making after *La Nuit américaine* he did not always succeed in choosing a subject and treating it in a way that pleased his most loyal followers, let alone a wider audience.

Yet, for me, at least four of the eight films he made after 1973 are outstanding. Of these *La Chambre verte* is particularly special, despite its morbid subject of obsession with the dead. His theme was that we forget all too soon those who have meant something in our lives. The writing of this book has been a way of giving substance to a memory. Ostensibly I have been writing about a film, but in the case of *La Nuit américaine* it is inseparable from its director. In the case of François Truffaut, and to answer his own question, his films and indeed cinema itself were not more important than life, though it was cinema that gave him a life. To some of us losing him meant losing a part of cinema. It cannot be regained, but it can be honoured.

LES FILMS DU CARROSSE
. . . .

Truffaut's filmography is unique for two reasons: first, every film he made was his choice, right from the beginning. Even Ingmar Bergman worked under contract for others in his early years. Second, with very few exceptions the films were made through his own company, Les Films du Carrosse, which was formed in 1957, the same year that Truffaut made the short *Les Mistons*.

It was his father-in-law, Ignace Morgenstern, who advised him to form a company. The advice included the use of Morgenstern's assistant, Marcel Berbert, who not only helped with the formal creation of the company, but, under instruction from Morgenstern, guaranteed first the production loan from the bank and then subsequently the laboratory costs of *Les Mistons*. It was not until years later that Truffaut learnt these facts.

Les Quatre cents coups (1959) was fifty per cent financed through one of Morgenstern's companies. The success of the film astonished his father-in-law, brought up on traditional fare. But it gave Truffaut the security he needed to continue to make films.

With the death of Morgenstern in 1961, Marcel Berbert became a permanent fixture at Carrosse as production executive, a role he continued

to fill until Truffaut's death. Incidentally, Berbert identified strongly with the portrait of childhood shown in *Les Quatre cents coups*, as his upbringing had been very similar.

In his piece in *Le Roman de François Truffaut*, Berbert, who plays one of the insurers alongside Graham Greene in *La Nuit américaine*, talks of the twenty years during which the door between his office and Truffaut's was never closed, unless one or the other had a visitor. The company, he says, never lost money on a Truffaut film. A record that must be unique in the history of cinema.

Suzanne Schiffman working with Truffaut on *Antoine et Colette*

Berbert also pays tribute to Suzanne Schiffman, who was always much more than just a script-girl, even before she achieved co-writer credit on *La Nuit américaine*. Suzanne was a fixture with the company from the time of *Tirez sur le pianiste* (1960) onwards. Apart from collaborating with Truffaut on the writing, she was trusted by him to handle much of the work of casting and location hunting.

This trio, augmented by regular co-writers such as Jean-Louis Richard or Jean Gruault and secretarial support were the true 'famille Carrosse'. The atmosphere associated with the company was not confined to the offices at 5 rue Robert-Estienne; Truffaut attached just as great importance to the needs of the extended family of cast and crew. Berbert describes the lengths that were gone to during the making of a film:

> On the shoots there were little parties, we brought discs and a record player from Carrosse, it was like a Saturday night dance. François feared that people would get bored when they passed four, six or ten weeks far from Paris. For the shoot of *Adèle H.* in Guernsey he took 16mm film prints and on Saturdays we organised screenings.[6]

Perhaps the most poignant portrait of working *chez* Truffaut is the one which is given by Truffaut's secretary, Josiane Couëdel, in her piece 'Fidèle, fidèle …' in *Le Roman de François Truffaut*. Couëdel was hired to take the place of Truffaut's secretary, Christine Pellé who wanted to work exclusively on continuity. Couëdel recounts how Truffaut disliked hierarchies. His strength lay in his ability to be able to relate to people – especially children – on their own level. She also describes how Truffaut was in the habit of asking the opinion of those around him regarding the quality of the script in development, and was always anxious about the response, needing to be reassured that it was being well received.

'François always presented me as "his big Breton secretary, with all that implies of character and temperament",' although she claims to be only one metre eighty in her very high heels. 'He often said to me in a tone of cheerful pride that he was my papa of Paris since my parents lived some way away.' She goes on to say:

> He loved to sing. When one mentioned Trenet, he never stopped, he knew all his songs by heart.

François was faithful, as in the song of Trenet, faithful without making a show of it, faithful also because he was scared of new faces. He created a world around himself. We were only three secretaries who worked successively for him. He kept contact because Christine Pellé remained his continuity girl and Lucette de Givray returned regularly to Carrosse for many years to archive old correspondence.[7]

Almost without exception Truffaut's employees ended up playing small parts in the movies, even shy Josiane Couëdel, who appears in *La Chambre verte* and *L'Homme qui aimait les femmes* (1977). It is odd to think of this in the light of the way people play themselves in *La Nuit américaine*.

If you examine the credits on Truffaut's movies there is further evidence of the 'family'. There are many assistants listed who are related to someone close to Truffaut. From André Bazin's son Florent to cameraman Henri Decae's daughter Jacqueline. When I was researching at Carrosse, editor Claudine Bouché's daughter was in the office checking some stills, and Madeleine Morgenstern reminded me that she had once been part of Nestor Almendros' crew on a Truffaut film.

In other circumstances this phenomenon of the close-knit film family would be considered nepotistic. But the truth is that, like Renoir, Truffaut saw film-making as an activity which you shared with people close to you, not as part of an industrial undertaking; and he would not have been able to work in any other way.

The actors in Truffaut's films are also part of the 'family'; they too are partners in the enterprise. Jacqueline Bisset remembers how grateful Truffaut was for the smallest bit of 'acting'. A quality she hasn't found in many other directors.

Truffaut was profoundly affected by the experience of acting for Steven Spielberg in *Close Encounters of the Third Kind*. It made him realise that the actor's life is one of continually wanting to please, and the need to know that you have achieved that objective; this thought is expressed by the character of Alexandre (Jean-Pierre Aumont) in *La Nuit américaine* when he says to Doctor Nelson:

As soon as we meet someone we ask ourselves: 'What does he think of me? Does he like me?' Oh, but I think it's the same for all artists!

18   Alphonse and Julie (top) imitate a moment in Truffaut's earlier film *Jules et Jim*

When Mozart was a child, and people would ask him to play he would answer: 'I'll play for you whatever you wish, but first tell me that you love me!'

For some years Truffaut developed the idea of a book on acting and actors. Sadly it never reached fruition, but the extent to which he admired and valued the contribution of the actor is abundantly clear. In many cases parts were written with an actor or actress in mind, and he claimed to be able to write better for an individual when working with them for the second time. He also said that you get to know the real actor in the editing room, when their every gesture and nuance of performance is anatomised by the process of cutting.

Like the fictional director in *La Nuit américaine*, it was Truffaut's habit to write dialogue the night before the scene was to be shot, or at the very least on the Sunday of the week in which a scene was scheduled. He was quite deliberately writing the words on the bodies of his actors. This is not unlike the feeling expressed by Robert Bresson when he refers to dreaming at night of the battles to be fought the following day, 'like Napoleon preparing his strategy on the bodies of his sleeping soldiers'. For Truffaut, the presence of the actors and their need to express the thoughts in the film had to coincide as much as possible with the moment when they were filmed, and not be something learned weeks before, like a stage performance.

Truffaut often referred to working with Jeanne Moreau on *Jules et Jim* (1962) as the most felicitous experience of his career. They established a lifelong friendship, and her intelligence as an actress must have been an early factor in foring his opinion of the supreme importance of the actor's role.

Moreau herself said that Truffaut didn't just understand women, he achieved a complicity with them. Martine Barraqué, who coincidentally took over the editing on his films starting with *L'Homme qui aimait les femmes* (*The Man Who Loved Women*), has said that she believes Truffaut would have been happy to have worked with an entirely female crew. In a strange way this confirms the notion of the family atmosphere unique to Truffaut and to the work of Carrosse.

GENESIS OF THE FILM
....

When the script of *La Nuit américaine* was published, François Truffaut wrote a foreword entitled, 'Cinema in Action'. He begins thus:

> In July 1971 I found myself in a state of exhaustion, both mental and physical. I had just finished shooting *Two English Girls* (*Deux Anglaises et le Continent*) and the sadness of the film had affected me. So, since my children were vacationing on the Riviera, I decided to have all the processed film sent down to Nice, where I could work on the editing in the more relaxed atmosphere of the Victorine Studios.[8]

It was at the Victorine Studios during the Second World War that Marcel Carné shot *Les Enfants du paradis* (1945). Like *La Nuit américaine*, this wonderful film also explores the world behind the scenes of a drama, although in this instance that of French Boulevard Theatre in Paris in the 1840s.

The script was by Jacques Prévert, who Truffaut much admired; in particular, he respected Prévert's ability to construct narratives around a considerable number of leading roles. Indeed, this was his own desire in *La Nuit américaine*, as up until then his films had been relatively simple stories with only three or four main characters.

Les Enfants du paradis opens, as does *La Nuit américaine*, with an elaborate street scene, constructed on the same back-lot as the one Truffaut would later use as the set for his film. In both films the milieu is presented with great élan through the opening sequence.

In 1971, what Truffaut encountered at the Victorine was the huge outdoor set that had been constructed in 1968 for the shoot of *The Madwoman of Chaillot*, directed by Brian Forbes and starring Katharine Hepburn. The set was still standing because the studio could not afford to have it dismantled.

When Truffaut first saw it it was 'already much the worse for wear, having been seriously damaged by the mistral wind and rain storms that sweep down over the Riviera from the Alps during the winter months'. A decaying set has it's own very particular appeal. There is a sense of past activity, of ghosts and images that once gave it life. For Truffaut it was an inspiration:

The more I looked the more interesting the set grew. In fact, it soon appeared most beautiful of all when viewed 'wrong side out'. It was then, I think, the idea hit me. A desire which had been playing around vaguely in the back of my mind for many years suddenly became crystallized: I would shoot a film about shooting a film – *a movie about film-making*.[9]

Truffaut's objective was:

To recount that formidable mobilisation that shooting a film involves, that input of feeling that can mess up the private lives of those who take part in a film. For each of us, at that particular moment, it is a privileged period having nothing to do with practical worries, an escape.[10]

Having determined on this 'movie about film-making' Truffaut spent a great deal of time exploring all the buildings that made up the Victorine Studios:

Already I had decided that if my story could take place entirely within this studio, I would have 'unity of place' without even half trying. 'Unity of time' resulted automatically, of course, given the premise of the shooting of a movie from the first day on the set until that final moment when the cast and crew disband. These two unities led, *a fortiori*, to the Aristotelian 'unity of action' as well.[11]

In Truffaut's mind there were risks associated with the film within the film. Indeed, for the dramatic theoretician, the 'unities' are denied by the existence of these two levels, even though we are concerned with the *creation* of the film within the film, rather than with the story itself. It was this aspect that drove him to state that he was not interested in, indeed was determined to avoid, creating any 'Pirandellian' conceits.

This I find perplexing. Pirandello, the Italian author (1867–1936), is most famous for his play *Six Characters in Search of an Author*. He was preoccupied by the shifting boundaries between illusion and reality, truth and make-believe, and the problems of personality and identity. Not only is a film about film-making unavoidably concerned with these issues, but it is difficult to understand why Truffaut would want to avoid them.

Certainly Truffaut's own concern with illusion and reality was a very serious one. He goes on to say in the foreword to the script, that:

> As a film-maker I have always been torn, on the one hand, by my hatred for the documentary ('the most false genre in all moviemaking' Jean Renoir rightly terms it) and, on the other, by my desire to use as the basis for all my scripts something which began as a real life fact.[12]

Truffaut needed to believe that his work reflected aspects of the human condition in a way that his audience could identify with, and just as he was interested in revealing the set 'wrong side out' so his characters needed to be seen when their private selves took over from the part they play in the film within the film.

Yet they are still performing roles. Truffaut and his collaborators on the script of *La Nuit américaine* were aware that however many masks you remove there is still one that remains. There are points in the writing and in the film's *mise en scéne* which seem deliberately contrived to make us feel that we are seeing the 'real' people behind the masks. They are rather like those very convincing photographs of people in the streets of Paris by Robert Doisneau, which give the illusion of spontaneity until we realise that all is not what it seems.

When Truffaut talks about the desire to portray his characters both on the set and in their private lives he refers to the fact that, 'As is usual in such cases, many of these characters would have some secret unknown to the others'.

Above all Truffaut was determined to do everything possible to convey the joy of film-making, an occupation which in his case was the centre of his existence. As he said:

> Moviemaking is a marvellous business, a wonderful craft. If anyone still needs proof of that, let him consider how of all those who have the good fortune to work in films not one ever wishes to do anything else! You may have heard of the great circus impresario, who, having gone bankrupt, ended up taking care of an acrobatic elephant who continually kicked him in the ass and who daily pissed in his face. One of the impresario's old friends, shocked at seeing him fallen so low, berated him: 'You have a

university degree and there's nothing you don't know about accounting! Why don't you get yourself a wonderful position in business administration?' To which he replied: 'And abandon show business? NEVER!'[13]

CREATING THE SCRIPT

. . . .

Suzanne Schiffman who received her first script credit on *La Nuit américaine*, has said that the first step for Truffaut in developing a script was to compile a dossier of notes and clippings relevant to the subject. Unfortunately, no dossier for *La Nuit américaine* has come to light despite careful searching of the Carrosse files; what I did find during my research were a few sheets of handwritten notes which had found their way into another file.

Suzanne Schiffman describes the next part of the process as creating a framework with a beginning, a middle and an end. In the case of *La Nuit américaine* the 'framework' took a unique form, as co-writer Jean-Louis Richard explains:

> For *La Nuit américaine* there was a big table in the house that we had rented in Antibes. We had discussions around this table in this rather sinister house, and one of us said: 'Hey! If we put a big roll of paper on the table we can write on it.' When we had an idea our problem was to integrate it at such and such a moment

On the wall: the actual treatment for *La Nuit américaine*

in the film, and then we would write it in the chosen place on the roll.[14]

It was believed that this outline for the film had also disappeared. Then, on my third visit to the offices of Carrosse, I spied something on the top of some shelves. When it was unrolled with the help of Madeleine Morgenstern, I realised I had seen it before: it is in the film, on the wall of the director Ferrand's room in the scene in which he is working on the script with Joëlle.

On the paper what were considered 'key' scenes are written in red, of which there are twelve. Other scenes are interspersed as satellites of each of these major sequences. This structure is traced entirely through scenes from 'Je vous présente Paméla'. All the activity off screen is built around the shoot. So the film within the film provides a scaffolding.

From this framework, a first draft was created. In the case of *La Nuit américaine* the first draft ran to over seventy pages. At the same time we are still a long way from the shooting script, a fact that is made abundantly clear by the proliferation of notes that appear in Truffaut's handwriting on his own copy.

The opening scene on the exterior set is described in detail. It is made clear that we should become quickly familiar with most of the main crew, and already, again in Truffaut's handwriting, there is the idea of establishing the wife of the production manager 'qui tricote dans un coin' (who knits in a corner).

The next section that is worth noting is the scene which includes the cat who doesn't like milk. As the director approaches the set he notices that one of the electricians is telling a story. He is persuaded to tell it to him too. It concerns an adventure he had the previous evening on the Croisette:

> on a bench, by the sea, he saw a woman, on her own; he sat down next to her and began to attract her attention. … The electrician was just about to take her off with him when she confessed falteringly, that she had swallowed a tube of gardenal an hour before, and that she was more or less on the point of dying!

Subsequently, we are in the rushes theatre viewing a scene based on the same story with Séverine becoming the woman who has taken an overdose. It is certainly believable that Séverine has become suicidal, since her husband has run off with her son's wife.

Later, when the older actress complains of the director using the make-up girl as an actress, Alexandre defends the director, saying that he approves of improvisation: 'The cinema was born in improvisation, it forced its invention; it petrifies each time it moves away from this and the cinema becomes inventive and alive again when it returns to its origins.'

When we find ourselves back in the cutting room watching the cut of the scene on the exterior set, it continues beyond the slap in the face, and we observe the son entering a porch where he starts to cry in the shadows. A concierge carries a bag of rubbish and pushes the timer light switch. The son leaves the porch, returns to the street and puts on a pair of glasses to hide his eyes. This elaboration would have spoilt the impact of the opening of the film.

The scene, 'La femme et le placard' (the woman and the cupboard), is here placed much later than in the finished film. It was the make-up girl on Martine Carol's last film who had told Truffaut about the trouble Carol had had both with her lines and a cupboard. At the end of the scene a way is found to substitute for Séverine's exit since she is incapable of opening the right door. Whilst the director is reassuring Séverine that everything will be fine and that she can return to her dressing room:

> The cameraman adjusts the lights so that the door closing can be suggested on the face of Alexandre. Everyone assists in realising this improvised shot, that is to say the script girl speaks the last line of Séverine out of shot; the chief electrician manoeuvres a 'flag' in front of a light which creates the effect of the shadow from the door on Alexandre's face, whilst an assistant closes a door from afar so that the soundman can record the right sound.

The shoot of the death of Julie (the son's wife) is described as: 'having the taste of an episode from Françoise Sagan: something between an accident and a suicide'. Sagan was a 60s icon; a novelist whose existential flavour encouraged a generation in France to live life to the full, with that philosophy's sense of fatalism.

This is a good example of how an early draft of a scenario can have interesting ideas which eventually have to be jettisoned. The most obvious example is the story told by the electrician and it's subsequent incorporation in the 'Pamela' script.

As we shall see with the final script of *La Nuit américaine* much was developed in the last phase. Perhaps this was often a result of the interaction between the words to be spoken and the action, but in a number of significant places whole new scenes were invented, which are not even hinted at earlier.

Opening Truffaut's copy of the shooting script provides an immediate surprise. It starts with a prologue:

CABINET DOCTEUR D'ASSURANCES. INT. JOUR

We are confronted by the director submitting to a medical prior to the film, to comply with insurance demands. The doctor passes comments on the fact that older directors have a fear of failing such a medical. He says: 'It is the point in common amongst all those who practice in the arts: no one envisages giving up, no one can accept the idea of being forced to retire.'

Suzanne Schiffman has said that she feels Truffaut would never have submitted to being seen naked on a couch; nor would he have considered retirement as giving up cinema would have been the same as giving up life.

The street scene is set out conventionally. It includes Alexandre telling Alphonse not to hesitate to hit him hard. 'The tears of Alphonse in the porch' is written in by Truffaut.

Ferrand is asked by the assistant director (Jean-François Stévenin), if he objects to a television interview. He replies that they can do what they like, as long as they take no image from the film itself.

Alexandre is interviewed then Alphonse takes his turn. Then comes Séverine, but her interview is crossed through by Truffaut. The decision to drop the interview with Séverine must have occurred late in the editing stage because two pages of sparkling dialogue were recorded in the post-sync session, during which Séverine expands on her reasons for not reading scripts or contracts. She admits to being so dedicated to creating characters that she is sometimes not sure where they end and the real person begins.

The interviewer flatters her by saying that everyone loves her and he believes that she loves the whole world in return. She tells him to beware, that she has to have a victim or bête noire on each film – as they say in french, 'une tête de turc'. She concludes by saying that he, the interviewer, is her 'tête de turc': everything will be his fault.

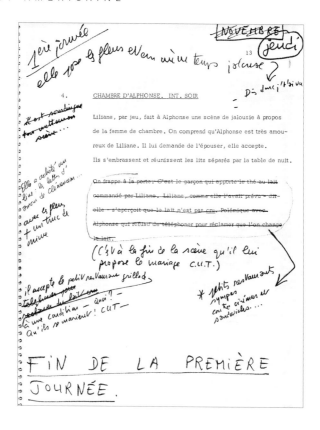

With everyone else she will act like an angel but to him she will be a monster!

When Ferrand meets Alphonse in the corridor with Liliane, the actor proposes that he move in the film like the young George Minafer Amberson in *The Magnificent Ambersons* and demonstrates his gait. Liliane comments that he looks like someone trying on a new suit at the tailors. This reference to a film by Orson Welles could have acted as a trigger to the nightmare where Ferrand dreams of stealing the stills from *Citizen Kane*. The dialogue was included in the post-sync session, which means it was shot, but eventually dropped from the cut.

The next scene conveys as clearly as any in the script the evolution of ideas. The detail is very specific. Thus, in Truffaut's handwriting

A simple scene but subject to Truffaut's constant search for significant detail and development

Liliane has not only bought a book, it is a specific book: *The Love Letters of Clemenceau*. Why Truffaut chose this particular book I have no idea; might it have meant something to a woman in his own life?

The section that is crossed out refers to Liliane ordering tea and complaining that the milk is not fresh. Not exactly special material, except, might we have compared it with the romanticism of the cat scene?

The following day two children are seen playing the card game 'Sept Familles Cinéma'. A variation of 'Happy Families', this was invented for the film and an enterprising company marketed the game after the film came out.

Later the camera crew are shooting some tests and Walter, the cameraman, is not happy with his assistant. In the dialogue that was post-recorded for the film he criticises the assistant's lack of speed and asks him: 'Is that what you learnt at Vaugirard?' This is a reference to the film school attended by Pierre-William Glenn the film's cinematographer. Truffaut remembered Glenn's less than humble attitude when he lectured there some years before, and this was his way of getting his own back, although, unfortunately, it didn't survive the editing.

When Bertrand (the producer) and Ferrand discuss the problem of Stacey's pregnancy there is a delicious moment that was excised from the final version. Bertrand says that Stacey is not the only problem. A writer published a novel called *Connaissez-vous Paméla*? some ten years ago, and is suing the production for three million old francs.

In reality, it was the writer of a novel called: *La Nuit américaine* who threatened to sue the production. However, Truffaut was able to show that he had established a legal right to the title before the novel was published. Life imitated art to the extent that the title was the only thing the film and novel had in common, the latter being about life in the Foreign Legion!

The conversation between Séverine and Julie about how she met Alphonse on holiday in Yorkshire and got to know him better because her cousin had chickenpox is handwritten by Truffaut. Thus he takes the opportunity to right the wrong done in his mind to Jacqueline Bisset in *Two For the Road* (1966) when she contracts chickenpox and loses Albert Finney to Audrey Hepburn.

What is more difficult to work out is Truffaut's choice of Yorkshire as a location. Truffaut's connection with Brontë country may well have been through his favourite painter, Balthus, who made an extensive series of engravings to illustrate *Wuthering Heights*. Truffaut had long wanted to make a documentary about the painter, but it was Pierre Zucca, Truffaut's stills man, who was to make a film on him some years later.

Next we cut to Alexandre telling Ferrand of his different screen deaths, in imitation of a speech Humphrey Bogart was fond of making to reporters.

During Stacey's departure for the TV job Alphonse talks to her about persuading Liliane to have a baby to cement their relationship. He tells her Liliane thinks it is irresponsible to have children in an age of atom bombs, pollution and drugs. Stacey will not interfere. Ferrand regrets that he will not be able to film her confinement, as he has always wanted to film a birth. This is a substantial scene which was removed from the final script.

According to Martine Barraqué the scene in which Séverine plays the woman who has taken poison was written by Truffaut to be shot in daylight and for Walter, the cameraman, to add the filter during the shot which would demonstrate the way 'day for night' is achieved. It was shot, cut and then dropped. Ironically this means that nothing in the finished film illustrates the technical connotation of the title.

When Ferrand and Joëlle work overnight on the script for the scene to be shot the following day, Truffaut has written that this is an opportunity to respond to objections to the subject of 'Je vous présente Pamela (tragédie bourgeoise)', and to confirm the origin of the subject: 'Father and son. A woman, recently married, meets her father-in-law and realises that the boy she has married is only a pale reflection of his father.' Joëlle comments that this sounds like a résumé one would read in *Pariscope* (the weekly guide to what is on in the French capital).

For the first time Ferrand calls into question the subject of the film that he is making. He picks up an evening paper, reads the headlines and comments: 'wouldn't it be preferable to make a film on the notary of Pezenas, the pollution, the strikes of Saint-Nazare etc?'

The approach to this scene demonstrates Truffaut's self-conscious attitude towards his material in relation to his audience and the critics. Martine Barraqué has said that Truffaut was fond of pre-empting his critics; whenever possible he would weave the perceived criticism into his films.

A note suggests that Truffaut was considering having the questions in the TV movie quiz about Renoir, and this connects with his original thoughts on the nightmare episode. His notes for this scene read: 'Ferrand returns to his bed. In the night a small boy (Christophe)

Stolen stills: souvenirs or inspiration?

cane in hand, approaches a cinema and steals 15 photos (*La Grande illusion?*...) ou (*Citizen Kane?*).' In the end his choice of *Citizen Kane* must have been dictated by the desire to communicate with a wider audience, but Renoir's classic would have been so apt since its title is also a metaphor for cinema.

At Alexandre's cocktail party Bertrand accepts to be interviewed by a critic, thus protecting Ferrand. A very elaborate conversation was recorded post-sync, so the scene was shot. The critic insists that all he and his fellow critics want is to *like* cinema. He implies that producers are out of touch with the tastes and concerns of ordinary people. Bertrand protests but the critic persists: if a film fails it is not the fault of the critics.

At the staging of the crash with the stuntman Truffaut writes that Alexandre coincidentally arrives in his car at the location with Christian. He has then crossed this out. Had it been left in, it would have given us an image of the two together in the car which later crashes – ironically where a crash is being staged.

The shoot of the false window proceeds without Alphonse. Truffaut writes that Walter, the cameraman, comments: 'Oh, that one is always in the salad, always in love.' Ferrand says that one day he is going to make a film called 'Les Salades de l'amour'. In this context 'salade' means mess-up. In a later film, *L'Amour en fuite* (1979), Truffaut has his hero Antoine Doinel write a book called 'Les Salades de l'amour'.

As Ferrand takes Alphonse back to his room the script does not include his speech about the nature of cinema as opposed to life. The craftsmanship of the writers has therefore to be admired for creating this piece on the spot.

For the scene of Julie in bed reading her lines Truffaut has written: 'chemise de nuit Dior' (Dior nightdress). He has also crossed through the words, 'attention soutien gorge et jupon …' ('pay attention to bra and slip …'). His concern for this kind of detail was almost obsessive; it is part of what made him such a special craftsman. It is also a measure of his preoccupation with all things female.

During the outburst from the wife of the production manager, Truffaut has written: 'Qu'est ce que c'est *ce* cinéma?' – an affectionate reference to André Bazin's collection of essays, *Qu'est que c'est le cinéma?*

Alexandre responds to the woman by saying that he doesn't think cinema is exceptional referring to his experience at the Ministry of

Agriculture, before he became an actor, where all the officials 'bathed in a climate of intrigue'. Truffaut has crossed out the sentence, 'it's like a compensation for the constraints of the world of civil servants'.

It was at the Ministry of Agriculture that Truffaut spent a few months after leaving the army. He therefore had first-hand knowledge on which to base this comparison. More importantly for his future career, the Ministry had a film library and a 16mm projector. When he wasn't busy putting labels on boxes he would run the films that interested him. Among these films was a short by Jacques Prévert.

The melodrama unravels in the shooting script as in the film until Julie's new lines based on her conversation with Ferrand are delivered to her dressing room. Truffaut admitted subsequently that his habit of borrowing from real life, even during the shoot of a film, began early in his career:

> That happens to me very often. I know that it is somewhat cruel. It is in fact a memory from *Jules et Jim*. Jeanne Moreau had a personal problem. She was very upset, she cried (there were no crying scenes in the film) and three days later I put this in a scene, the one in which she and Oscar Werner cry together, and I gave them several lines that she had spoken when she was upset. But in the end, in this film it was meant to illustrate an important part of the work of the director, that is to steal.[15]

He could have added, not only from life but also from other movies.

FROM SCRIPT TO SCREEN
· ·

The process of writing the script continued from early 1971 until shooting was completed in November 1972. In between Truffaut conceived, shot, edited and released Une Belle fille comme moi. This film opened in Paris a mere fortnight before shooting started in Nice on *La Nuit américaine*. The gestation of a film was not always as direct as Truffaut had once described it to Josiane Couëdel: 'Like the nine months of a pregnancy'.

Yet some aspects of the production were simpler than usual. The shoot was virtually self-contained at the studios. On the other hand a great deal of the budget had to be allocated to making good the set of the 'Parisian square'.

Significantly the only change to the crew from the previous film was to replace Jean-Pierre Kohut with Damien Lanfranchi as art director. Lanfranchi was introduced to Marcel Berbert, production controller at Les Films du Carrosse, in the spring of 1972, by a location manager who had worked with both him and Truffaut in Nice. Lanfranchi had worked as assistant art director on *The Madwoman of Chaillot* in 1968, and was by now an established designer. He therefore

Truffaut and the art director, Damien Lanfranchi, examine the design for the lovers' bungalow

knew not only the studio and its staff but he was familiar with the large exterior set:

> I supervised the revamping of the big exterior set. I did not have any assistant or draughtsman at all, all through the preparation and the shooting. Every set was decided accordingly with F. Truffaut and all the departments concerned: camera and lighting department included.[16]

That Lanfranchi should work unaided as designer, art director and draughtsman would shock any equivalent craftsman in Hollywood or Britain used to a large team on any major feature film. This gives some indication of the skeleton crew that Truffaut had become accustomed to. This was not only practical in terms of budgetary constraints but was clearly the way the director preferred to work.

It was after using Pierre-William Glenn as cinematographer on *Une Belle fille comme moi* that Truffaut decided to continue with him on *La Nuit américaine*. In a letter to Nestor Almendros, whom he had used previously, he explained:

> Despite the admiration and friendship which I carry for you, I am going to shoot my next film with the same camera crew (Glenn, Bal, Khripounoff) and also two others in addition, because we are going to shoot with 3 or sometimes 4 cameras. Also I am going to simplify it in order to shoot in six weeks with this re-inforced crew. It is another work compared with what we have done together with *L'Enfant* or *Les Anglaises* a different enterprise.[17]

Glenn was presented with the difficult task of lighting to accommodate shooting with several cameras, with at least one view needing to include the scene being shot for 'Je vous présente Paméla' and the camera filming that scene. Truffaut had to know that his alternative points of view were all usable to allow the final structure to emerge in the editing of the film.

Glenn was working with colour stock rated at only 50 ASA: a very slow speed compared with today when directors of photography are used to 200 ASA and above. This slow stock required considerably more lighting, the preparation of which was time-consuming.

Casting proved a complicated matter. On a handwritten sheet describing the individual characters, the only time when an actor's name is mentioned is for Alexandre, called 'le père'. Truffaut has written Charles Boyer, Louis Jordan and finally Jean-Pierre Aumont. Boyer was perhaps Truffaut's ideal, but Aumont was no third-rate substitute.

Truffaut described Aumont as having the 'perfume of Hollywood' and representing the 'mythology of cinema'. Indeed Aumont had worked in Hollywood alongside Ginger Rogers, Jean Simmons, and with his compatriot Leslie Caron in *Lili* (1952). His career in French cinema was well established even before the Second World War, in such films as *Drôle de drame* (1937) and *Hôtel de Nord* (1938).

In a letter to Aumont, a few months before shooting began, Truffaut describes himself as enchanted by Aumont's memoirs, *Souvenirs provisoires*, especially the section on Aumont's second wife, Maria Montez, who had been a particular favourite of Truffaut's when he had been growing up. Truffaut also mentions having very much enjoyed meeting his choice for the part of Séverine, Valentina Cortesa: 'a real character, extremely feminine and very funny'.

Cortesa's experience in Hollywood and Europe made her the ideal choice for the role. She had been directed by Jules Dassin and Robert Wise in America and had played opposite James Stewart and Spencer Tracy. In Italy she had worked with Antonioni, Fellini and Zeffirelli; she was also well known in the theatre, working mainly with her husband Georgio Streller who ran the Piccolo Teatro di Milano. In fact she postponed her appearance there in *Anthony and Cleopatra* to accept the role in *La Nuit américaine*, making the comment that her Cleopatra was no longer a young woman and could wait another year.

Jean-Pierre Léaud had always been the only choice for Alphonse. Despite the reference to the character having started as a jockey and then studied mime, there is no doubt that Léaud is playing himself or the actor who played Antoine Doinel.

The casting of Jacqueline Bisset seems to have been Truffaut's preference, even though – most unusually for him – he had never met her. Bisset thought the whole process was very 'haphazard':

> I later found out that I had been enquired after by François a year before I was sent the script. … I was actually in Paris living la vie de Bohème … how I was tracked down was an absolute mystery to me.[18]

Some time after Bisset had returned to California her participation was confirmed:

> he [Truffaut] met me at the airport with an enormous bunch of gladioli, almost as big as he was. He was very formal. ... He had his own agenda: I had no idea why I was cast; I certainly didn't feel like the Hollywood actress.[19]

Truffaut himself said that he was 'conquered' by her in Donen's *Two For the Road* (1966). He claimed that since seeing the film in 1967 not a week had passed without him wondering why wasn't it Audrey Hepburn [and not Bisset] who got the chickenpox.

For the part of the continuity girl, Joëlle, Truffaut clearly had Suzanne Schiffman in mind as the model. The casting of Nathalie Baye came about as the result of a coincidence. Baye had recently graduated from the *conservatoire* and had acquired an agent, Serge Rousseau, who had played a small part in *Baisers volés* (1968). Rousseau was married to Marie Dubois who was the girl befriended by Charles Aznavour in *Tirez sur le pianiste*. Nathalie Baye was spotted by Suzanne Schiffman walking on the street with Rousseau near Truffaut's office. Schiffman, having just been told about the part by Truffaut, rang Rousseau and asked if the girl she had seen him with was an actress. Learning that she was, Schiffman arranged for her to meet Truffaut. Baye recalls:

> and we talked together ... and he said, I'm very pleased to meet you but you're not really for the part ... when he wrote the script he thought of Suzanne ... and Suzanne was more ... er ... with short hair ... a little like a boy you know ... but anyway he said come up again tomorrow ... and he asked me to read a scene with him ... I didn't really realise it was an audition ... and he said okay ... so he took his glasses and put them on my nose ... and he said you're going to work in glasses.[20]

Baye and Truffaut became close friends and starred together in what was probably Truffaut's most personal film, *La Chambre verte*. For her *La Nuit américaine* was an auspicious start to a wonderful career.

It is not clear what criteria were used to decide which of the crew roles should be played by actors. Considering the difficulty that Valentina Cortesa had with knowing 'who is a make-up girl and who is an actress', the part taken by Nike Arrighi was perhaps a marginal decision: a fact confirmed by Suzanne Schiffman who told me that the original thought was for the real make-up girl to double in the part. This would not have been surprising since Thi Loan N'Guyen, one of the actual make-up artists on the shoot, subsequently acted in a number of Truffaut's films. In the end, says Schiffman, this idea was considered impractical and Arrighi was chosen.

Born in Nice, the daughter of an Italian count and an Australian ballerina, Arrighi could speak Italian, French and English and thus was able to converse with the various cast members in their native tongue. She was a graduate of The Royal Academy of Dramatic Art in London, and had appeared in a number of British films. (Her first appearance in front of a camera was in the first film I ever edited: a short called *The Market*, directed by Ron Porter.)

The part of the stagiaire attached to Joëlle to learn continuity was given to Dani (Danièle Graule). She was in the habit of collecting her small boy from the nursery school at the end of rue Robert-Estienne and it was Truffaut himself who spotted her outside his office.

Alexandra Stewart, who plays Stacey, the pregnant secretary, had already appeared in Truffaut's *La Mariée etait en noir*. They had been very close at that time. Born in Montreal, Alexandra had come to Paris to perfect her French. By the late 50s she had begun to work in cinema and had many credits to her name by the time Truffaut first used her in 1967. Truffaut had proposed her for the part of Bonnie when he was contemplating making *Bonnie and Clyde* in 1965.

It was as a result of seeing Bernard Menez's performance in his début film at a screening at the Cinématheque, that Truffaut decided to engage him for the important role of the propsman. His rather quirky presence suited the desire to emphasise the importance of this function. Truffaut quoted Fernandel in Marcel Pagnol's *Le Schpountz* who said, in the character of an *accessoiriste*: 'we don't appreciate propmen enough … a badly chosen teapot can totally spoil a love scene.'

In casting David Markham as Doctor Nelson, Truffaut used an English actor whom he was familiar with from his appearance as the 'palmiste' in *Les Deux anglaises et le continent*, in which his daughter, Kika, had played one of the two heroines.

For the part of the producer Truffaut chose to break from the clichéd image of that role by choosing Jean Champion, a 'mild and warm' actor, whom he had admired both in Alain Resnais' *Muriel* (1963) and on the stage in Chekhov's *The Three Sisters*.

As regards the small parts, what is apparent is that some were cast on the spot. The young man, Christian, whom Alexandre wants to adopt, just happened to be visiting his girlfriend, Nathalie Baye, on the shoot. Baye told me that Jean-Pierre Aumont took a liking to him and that was that.

The most bizarre piece of casting, however, was that of Graham Greene, alongside Truffaut's head of production, Marcel Berbert, as one of the 'English insurers'. Greene was a friend of Michael Meyer, who knew Nike Arrighi. During the shoot Meyer and Arrighi went to see Graham Greene, who lived just along the Riviera at Antibes. Meyer had already been rejected by Truffaut for the part of the insurer, because he looked 'too intellectual'.

When Greene heard this he wondered whether Truffaut would consider him for the part. He was introduced incognito as Henry Graham to Suzanne Schiffman. She said she would 'control' with Truffaut, and pointed Greene out across the room. Truffaut gave his approval. Schiffman mentioned that for small parts like this there was no money, only signed copies of Truffaut's books. It was agreed that this would be alright as Mr 'Graham' had a pension!

Apparently Greene had cold feet the next day, not wanting the press to get hold of the story. But he was persuaded that he should fulfil his 'contract' as they had no time to recast.

On the day the scene was to be shot everyone, especially Arrighi, was apprehensive. She remembers being in the make-up room when Schiffman burst in and said that Truffaut had recognised Greene and was furious. In fact Truffaut, who loved practical jokes, played along with things until the scene was in the can, and then embraced the writer. They subsequently became good friends and at one point discussed making a film together.[21]

Greene always hated being filmed, certainly as himself, and he was not very well served by the adaptations of his works for the screen, but he had a lifelong love of the cinema, and had been an eminent critic in the 1930s for *The Spectator*. A remark he had made about Shirley Temple whilst writing for another journal, *Night and Day*, had led to a libel suit and the closure of that magazine. He thus shared the outspokenness of Truffaut's critical past. They might well have made very good collaborators.

So that is the story behind the casting, except … well, there is an undated handwritten note of Truffaut's, on paper from the Century Hotel in Antwerp, which lists Jean Servais or Michel Bouquet as the father, and Serge Rousseau as the husband. It even suggests that Alexandra (Stewart) would play the stagiaire. On another similar sheet, most eminent middle-aged French actors of the time are listed, except that is Jean-Pierre Aumont. The list also includes Marie Dubois (script-girl?) and 'l'italienne Sylvana' (Mangano?), the latter perhaps an early idea for Séverine.

If I read his notes correctly, it was Jean-Claude Brialy who Truffaut had in mind for the director before he convinced himself that he should play the part. We have to say that this was a felicitous decision, and that only his total trust in Suzanne Schiffman as the surrogate director made it possible.

In an interview in 1974, Truffaut had the following to say about casting, knowing the actors and the effect on the script, especially the dialogue:

> I'm very fond of making up dialogues in the course of shooting, when I've come to know my actors better. I can follow better what the film is becoming from the way the actors react. For almost all the films I do just that. All the same there is the drawback of making scenes a little too short during the filming, because it happens that one says to oneself: 'If we shoot more than two pages, the actor will not be able to remember it all,' and so one makes the scenes a little short.[22]

Truffaut loved dialogue and considered it to be a crucial part of cinematic expression. He was always determined to integrate his conception of each character, and the lines they would speak, with the personality of the actor he had cast. He said of working on *La Nuit américaine*: 'there were many actors I didn't know. So I discovered them in the course of shooting and with that as a basis, wrote their texts every Sunday for the next week on the set.'[23]

There is no doubt that Jacqueline Bisset found this as hard in practice as it is implied in the film. She was totally lost off the set when everybody was talking French: 'They just jabbered on and I couldn't understand a word.'

As the casting proceeded the finance for the film was put in place, though not without some difficulty. Marcel Berbert produced an estimated budget of three and a half million francs: which was a very reasonable sum for a script that demanded several stars and a complicated shoot.

Nevertheless, Les Artists Associés, Truffaut's usual source of funding, refused to finance the picture, judging the script to be too intellectual and thus too risky. In particular, they mistrusted the concept of having a film within the film which they felt might be disconcerting for the average audience.

Berbert took the project to Robert Solo, the representative for Warner Bros. in London, through the assistant in Paris, Simon Benzakein. Solo, an admirer of Truffaut, gave his approval in principle in November 1971. The contract was finally signed in May 1972. The budget was, however, tight and this was to have an effect on the schedule. Apparently $100,000 that had been assumed to be secure, was not forthcoming. When this was learned part way through filming, a week had to be dropped from the shooting schedule.

In September 1972 the cast and crew assembled in Nice. It was a busy time for the Victorine Studios: Herbert Ross was directing a film starring James Mason, and, more pertinently, Nathalie Delon was also making a picture there. Before long, friendly relations were established, especially between the crews. So much so that some found it hard to get to the set after socialising the night before, despite the fact that shooting often didn't start before midday.

This late start was not unusual; at the time it was traditional for the working day on French films to run from 12 noon to 7 p.m. According to Schiffman, Truffaut used the mornings to work out his shooting plan, which he never did before being on the specific location or set. Just as dialogue was left to be determined by reacting to the actors, so Truffaut reacted to the space for a scene before knowing where to put the camera and how to stage the action.

Yet he had an instinct for the right shot. He knew that point-of-view was the key to *mise en scène*. He also knew the frame without looking through the camera. Suzanne Schiffman was told by one of his cameramen that no director he had worked with knew so clearly where he wanted the camera. Not only this, but Truffaut was apparently always right.

Damien Lanfranchi, the art director, told me that this was

The only movie on which I never heard any discussion or debate about the camera position. He used to have in his pocket small pieces of paper with camera angles, lenses, details of each scene, sketched out before with Suzanne Schiffman.[24]

The director of photography, Pierre-William Glenn, points out that Truffaut hardly ever varied the camera angle on a scene by more than 30 to 40 degrees between shots. Often there is almost no change at all when he moves in for closer shots. This is a deliberate and significant aspect of his style. In *La Nuit américaine* there are some notable exceptions, but they are always due to the need to show both the action and the camera and crew shooting it.

Careful examination of the production reports reveals that for almost half the scenes in *La Nuit américaine* only one shot was made. Even more remarkably, for many of these only one or at the most two takes were made of this single shot. This is the clearest factual indication we have of Truffaut's cinematic sureness.

The disadvantage of this technique is that there is enormous pressure on finding the right angle. But the bonus is a clear and deliberate point-of-view which gives the audience the security that Truffaut felt was paramount in cinematic storytelling.

Some if not all of his other preferred directors, for instance Renoir and Lubitsch, certainly tended towards the same direct and uncomplicated use of the camera. Even such seemingly different directors as Bergman and Buñuel were in favour of a careful choice of the single point-of-view. The virtue of Buñuel and Renoir, which I am sure Truffaut admired, was their preference for doing the right shot once, even if it was technically imperfect, rather than attempting the wrong shot ten times. As Truffaut said:

Everything depends on what you consider important. For my part I am only bothered with what I am responsible for. If an actor acts badly, it's my fault. If the film comes back from the laboratory scratched, that's not my fault. It's my work that is important. In any case, after eight days of showing, the film will be scratched, so I don't even redo that take. A travelling shot trembles, that's of no importance. What is, is knowing whether the travelling shot was necessary, whether it looks good, what it brings to the film. If it trembles that's too bad.[25]

The effectiveness of this particular shoot depended on one other person: Jean-François Stevenin, credited as assistant director alongside Suzanne Schiffman, and performing that role both in front of and behind the camera. He was to act again for Truffaut; as the schoolteacher in *L'Argent du poche* (1976). His affection for Truffaut is apparent in his piece in *Le Roman de François Truffaut*:

> The rapport he had with his crew on *La Nuit américaine* corresponded exactly with that which he had with us during the shoot. He was very alone and separated from the crew, but the parties during the shoot had as their goal a compensation for this isolation. On *La Nuit américaine* there was a party every three days until about six o clock in the morning. He, who never drank a drop, stayed around, acting the host. The parties became part of the film; family parties where everything happened according to a code. Truffaut had a very subtle ability to hold everyone in his hands. He imposed his authority without demanding anything; a great art. …
> I was faithful to my position and ready for everything.[26]

Shooting started on 25 September 1972. The schedule was only adhered to for the first two days. In feature film production it is not unusual for there to be some variation from the schedule and there can be many causes; from bad weather postponing the shooting of exteriors, to accidents and the unavailability of actors. In the case of *La Nuit américaine* the variation was considerable.

After spending the first four days on minor scenes the fifth day was entirely devoted to the crowd scene in the 'Parisian square'. It took ten takes of the master shot to satisfy Truffaut and his crew, so the montage of clapperboards in the film is an accurate representation of the real shoot. There are few scenes of this complexity in Truffaut's films and the added complication of the multiple cameras must have made each take a minor military operation.

An examination of the call sheet for this scene reveals just how complicated a shoot it was. Apart from the principals and the cameo roles, 200 extras were called 'to circulate in the square'. Of the crew, not only was everything doubled, but a 'prop' crew was hired to cover the additional mock cameras. The long prop list includes 'spectacles for the script-girl' and 'knitting for the wife of the production manager'.

The lovers' bungalow was the only scene covered on the sixth day. It was subsequently re-shot three times; that is, re-takes and additional shots for a final total of twenty slates. On the screen it is difficult to perceive why this particular scene should have been so much trouble. But what we should remember is that it included the story told to Ferrand by the electrician from Marseille which was subsequently dropped.

After a day off on Sunday 1 October, the shoot returned momentarily to the scenes as scheduled. In this case the children playing the card game 'Sept Familles Cinéma' (one shot) and the cocktail party when the stuntman arrives. On the Tuesday, also as scheduled, the stunt was shot. This adherence to plan obviously coincided with the availability of 'Mark Spencer'. The stunt was marred by an injury to a member of the crew, as it is reported in the production notes that at 16.55: 'Louis Cardelli (chef machiniste) se blessé à la tête ... en montant, le matériel – chute de pierres.'

When the discussion between Bertrand and Alexandre subsequent to Madame Lajoie's outburst about the morality of film people was filmed, it included a speech from Bertrand detailing the sexual intrigues between members of staff of various Paris métro stations, which used station names in place of people's names:

> take the people who work on the Métro with their unsociable hours, and listen to them, let them speak, the drivers and ticket collectors: Vaugirard is no longer with Censier-Daubenton, she has gone off with Lamarck-Caulaincourt, you know that Monge is cuckolded by Muette, Marcel-Sembat has made a kid with Solferino, Hôtel de Ville was going to marry Cardinal-Lemoine, but Pyramides surprised him in a hotel room with Chaussée d Antin.

At the end of this week the crew assembled in the evening for the night shoot of the encounter in the kitchen in which Alexandre and Julie confess their love. It was in the can by 1.15 in the morning.

The first two days of the following week were devoted to Séverine's major scene. Nineteen shots were taken. On the first day a crew member, José Bois, burnt his right hand and arm, presumably whilst igniting the gas fire.

Although bad weather and the occasional accidents intervened the shoot proceeded smoothly despite Truffaut deciding to re-shoot or obtain more shots for a substantial number of scenes. Nothing was left unshot apart from the medical examination.

There is, however, one remaining mystery: Ferrand's nightmare of the small boy stealing stills from *Citizen Kane* was not in the schedule. Indeed the only mention of it is in Truffaut's script in his own handwriting, labelled '32bis'. Nor is there any note of the boy among the cast detailed on the schedule.

The editing period of *La Nuit américaine* was the longest of any Truffaut film according to Martine Barraqué. She also remembers that after the film opened in Cannes, Truffaut said in a radio interview that he could not have done it without the help of an editor as good as Yann Dedet.

Why was it so difficult to cut? The answer lies primarily in the problem posed by the film within the film, and the construction of many scenes with two, sometimes three points-of-view to be considered, thus doubling and sometimes trebling the alternatives.

This was the eighth film of Truffaut's which Yann Dedet had worked on, and his third as editor with Martine Barraqué as his assistant, so they were familiar with each other and with Truffaut's method.

For both Dedet and Barraqué the experience of cutting *La Nuit américaine* was a joy, despite the very long schedule. Truffaut was in a very positive mood though this did not prevent his usual anxiety about keeping the film moving. This meant that some scenes had to be dropped; for instance the conversation between Ferrand and Stacey about wanting to film a confinement, which was shot twice and cut but failed to meet with Truffaut's satisfaction.

The director's anxiety also meant that Dedet was forced to tighten each scene and to intercut more than was necessary. Most noticeably the junctions of scenes are very sharp, leaving only the kernel of each scene in the film. For Dedet this was sometimes too much for his taste:

> François always wanted to be faster in movies. He said life is annoying and in a movie you can correct this by going fast. Martine tried better than me to instill some silence in the later films, which was very difficult because he always wanted to speak the text incessantly.[27]

This desire for a fast pace must have meant that many scenes were re-cut, even when they were perfectly edited, simply to inject more 'dynamism' into the narrative. This is apparent from the first big scene and the montage of 'claps' used to emphasise the repetition of the shot.

I believe Truffaut's love of dynamic cutting is one of his great strengths, and it serves him well most of the time. For an example in his later work examine the exposition of *La Femme d'à côté*. It is as good as anything in Hitchcock, which Truffaut would accept as the ultimate accolade. However, he was not usually making a thriller, and a quieter rhythm, perhaps borrowed from Renoir, would have been at times more appropriate.

That Truffaut's attitude to editing was derived from his desire to succeed with his audience is made obvious from his own comments on the subject. For instance, the following which was cited by Claude de Givray in 1966:

> I work for the public of the Cineac-Saint-Lazare, for the viewer that pops in to watch a bit of the film distractedly before catching his train. ... Considering that people lock themselves up in the dark

The editors, Yann Dedet and Martine Barraqué, working with Ferrand (Truffaut)

to see my films, I never fail at the end of a film to take them out into nature, to the seashore or into the snow, to get myself pardoned.[28]

He was aware that the editing stage was crucial:

> I get to understand certain things only at the editing table: in *La Nuit américaine* for example, important decisions were made rather late. Editing is a very creative period because, as a rule, you can't afford to blunder. A film can get ruined in the editing, but generally you do it a lot of good.[29]

The editing was finished in time to print the film for the opening of the 1973 Cannes Film Festival, but not before Truffaut's long-time collaborator, Georges Delerue, had contributed an excellent score. It was in describing his attitude to the music that Truffaut revealed his true intention with *La Nuit américaine*:

> In *La Nuit américaine* I used it solely for the scenes at work, because I felt that the true subject was work and that, in the

The composer Georges Delerue acting for Truffaut in *Les Deaux anglaises et le Continent*   47

moments that work was no longer shown as realistic but as narrative, the work itself had to be glorified at these moments. It was the subject: the idea that all those people that you see are stronger at work.[30]

Certainly this view corresponds with the feelings of Georges Delerue:

The film of François' that moves me most is perhaps *La Nuit américaine*. This hymn of love to cinema resembles him most, it was all his life, his passion. This scene at the end where everyone goes their separate ways after the shoot is so true! The emotion of this 'famille du spectacle' that is saying goodbye always gets to me. If François has shot it like this it is because after each film he became upset and sad. This scene is superb, all the decency and emotion of François can be found there.[31]

AN ANATOMY OF THE FILM

. . . .

During my interview with the editors, Dedet and Barraqué, I reminded them about the director's medical examination scene which was scripted to open the film. They both said that they could not imagine *La Nuit américaine* beginning in any other way than it does, that is with the soundtrack visible alongside the opening credits.

The soundtrack we 'see' is a montage of the orchestra being put through its paces – from Vivaldi to *bal musette* – by the composer Georges Delerue, whose voice and baton we hear punctuating the music. The inclusion of the optical soundtrack in the frame is the aural equivalent of shooting off the edge of the set which occurs at the end of the first scene. The audience is immediately aware that it is going to experience the world beyond the frame.

The pull-out on the image of the Gish sisters is made in reverential silence; only at the end does Truffaut's voice speak the dedication as it appears, in his own handwriting, on the screen. In his review of Otto Preminger's *Bonjour Tristesse* in 1958 Truffaut wrote:

Truffaut's dedication to the Gish sisters

> Cinema is the art of the woman, that is of the actress. The director's work consists in getting beautiful women to do beautiful things. For me, the great moments of cinema are when the director's gifts mesh with the gifts of an actress.[32]

Oddly enough, no such pairing of director and actress is obvious with Truffaut himself; even Jeanne Moreau had already acquired such status with Louis Malle in *Les Amants* (1958) before she first starred for Truffaut in *Jules et Jim*.

It was not for want of trying: from his early film *Les Mistons*, which opens with a montage of Bernadette Lafont cycling in the summer sun, to his last film, *Vivement Dimanche*, which begins with a celebration of his last love, Fanny Ardant, as she walks elegantly and sensuously along a Parisian street, Truffault's camera never failed to worship his female stars. He gave a further explanation of the Gish dedication in 1980:

> Sadness without end are films without women! I detest war films except for the moment when a soldier takes a woman's photo from his pocket to admire. D. W. Griffith was the first to realise that films were the art of woman, the art of showing women. When the talent scouts of Hollywood were running around the United States, practising the slogan: 'Cherchez-la-femme', Griffith himself had no need to seek he had found ... Lilian Gish.[33]

As if to rupture our worship of the female star the film makes a hard cut to a sun-lit Parisian square, and we are immediately immersed in a typically French scene, but also in a piece of cinema. The dedication actually prepares the audience to be transported into the world that Truffaut has prepared for us. What we are faced with is an everyday scene in Paris until the young man slaps his father's face. The shock of this action is compounded by the shout of 'coupé' from the director as the mechanics of cinema are revealed.

A frame by frame analysis of this scene reveals considerable discontinuity, all of which is elided by the pace and skill of the editing. The final shot is neither from the position used for the 'real' shot, this camera never being visible although its tracks are clearly in position, nor from the crane that we see in the shot.

The artfulness of the opening scene is that it manages to convey various details of the film crew in action at the same time as introducing the individual members of both cast and crew and giving us an outline of the story of the film within the film.

This clever exposition continues on the landing of the hotel as the director deals with questions from his colleagues. Liliane remarks on Ferrand's deafness, and Alphonse explains that it happened when the director was in the artillery – a reference to Truffaut whose hearing was affected in the same way while in the army. Truffaut later explained that he decided upon this feature of Ferrand to give him a distinguishing charcacteristic without falling into the usual clichés associated with directors; preferring the prop of a hearing aid to a beard or moustache or a distinctive style of dress: a distinguishing characteristic which, moreover, associates the character with Truffaut himself.

The jealousy provoked in Liliane by Alphonse eyeing the chambermaid leads to her remark about jealousy being absurd unless you go the whole way and commit murder. This reminds us of Truffaut's *La Peau douce* (1964) in which the wife takes revenge on her erring husband, an incident which was based on a true story, as was the plot of 'Paméla'.

As the young couple put their beds together, we enjoy the exchange about how it is impossible from Alphonse's point-of-view, and we might add Truffaut's, in a town with thirty-seven cinemas, to talk about restaurants. Indeed in Nice it is very easy to talk about and enjoy at least thirty-seven *restaurants*. No doubt these days, there are far fewer cinemas to enjoy.

Truffaut takes a simple and for him typical approach to the shooting of this scene. There are no perceptible changes of angle; only a number of cuts to closer or wider shots, enabling Yann Dedet to incorporate sections of different takes where he and Truffaut felt that performance was better, or simply to affect the dynamic.

The scene in the bedroom concludes with Alphonse proposing to Liliane, as he mimes with an imaginary flower, acceding to her request to eat out. She does not reply and the image slowly fades out. Truffaut always enjoyed the use of visual effects to emphasise a moment, especially when delicate emotions were involved. It is an echo of the silent era; indeed Lilian Gish must have held a look many times as the camera operator faded out in the camera. The fade out on this Liliane is accompanied by a rather mournful, almost foreboding moment of music.

The director is confronted by problems as he progresses across the back-lot. The camerawork is hand-held and was originally all one shot. Several cuts have been made to alter the order of the encounters. The addition of Truffaut's voice-over comparing the shoot to a perilous journey across the Old West helps weld the sequence.

Each encounter has a point. The choice of car for the stunt shows that the director is so focused on the needs of the film that he does not hesitate to choose a car belonging to a member of the crew.

With the designer, played by the real art director Damien Lanfranchi, Ferrand is at pains to avoid unnecessary work and cost by not wanting the interior of the lovers' bungalow to be practical, since he only wants to shoot from the outside. We are, as always, dealing with a façade.

His encounter with the producer underlines the need to be flexible within the parameters of the finance available. Although it is noticeable that Ferrand talks about a five-day working week when in fact the crew worked six days most of the time.

The rushes screening was placed much later in the script. Brought forward it gives the feeling that we are in the midst of the shoot since material is viewed other than that of the crowd scene. Instead it is the moment Alphonse tells his mother that he is 'going to kill them both', which originally we were supposed to see as a scene being shot.

With very few exceptions rushes viewing theatres in film studios are cramped spaces designed for no more than a handful of viewers. The one at the Victorine was no exception, as can be judged on the screen, and which I can vouch for from my own visit not long after *La Nuit américaine* was made. (At the time I can remember realising with a surprising frisson that I was sitting in the seat which had been occupied by Alphonse.)

It is here, in the screening room, that the first test of the progress of a film is made, after the laboratory has rendered visible the images committed to celluloid.

These occasions can be very tense. It is a measure of the closeness of the 'Paméla' team that everyone attends; except Séverine who 'never comes to rushes', presumably due to her neurotic aversion to watching her own performance – not wanting to be undermined by viewing material in its raw state, which is often far more disturbing than when cut together.

This projection was to have included the screen test made by Stacey. I regret that we are denied this, if only because screen tests are a particularly strange phenomenon, often being so artificial as to be of

little use in judging an actor's potential. In any case Truffaut seldom resorted to them, an exception being when he was casting the lead in *Les Quatre cents coups* and discovered Jean-Pierre Léaud.

From the point when Alexandre enters Séverine's dressing room, to the moment he closes the door as he leaves, there is only one cut away to Odile from the master shot, which may well have allowed the use of a different take for the second half. The energy is in the performances, and not cutting serves to enhance the impression of immediacy.

This scene makes no sense in terms of continuity. The scene with Alphonse that Séverine is supposed to be playing that day has already been seen in the rushes screening immediately before. The fact that Alexandre says that they are not playing together that day is denied subsequently because they are on the set with each other. Such obvious temporal lapses in continuity never seemed to disturb Truffaut, concerned as he was with other levels of meaning and emotion.

The scene where we see Séverine having a problem with her lines and not knowing which door to exit from is nearly nine minutes long; and if this was all that Truffaut had committed to celluloid about the joy and pain of film-making it would be enough.

First we are reminded of cinema as illusion as the artificial fire is tested. Truffaut takes the opportunity to compare television to the flickering fire that humanity has always needed as a distraction, especially after dinner! The trouble is that a fire leaves scope for the imagination, whereas television merely dulls the brain.

The director is then confronted by a German 'talent' agent and his protégées, two strapping women. The agent proceeds to cross-examine him as to why he has made neither political nor erotic films.

Truffaut was often criticised for a lack of political engagement in his films. He was genuinely disinterested, and felt that it was wrong to use the medium to sermonise. That he should bracket political with erotic films is odd except that sexual politics had become a strong agenda during the 60s. His own eroticism was always a matter of allusion with the one exception of the powerfully effective scene in *Les Deux anglaises et le Continent* where the loss of Anne's virginity is graphically conveyed.

He is dragged away from this confrontation by a considerate Jean-François, forever protective of his director. Unfortunately he then runs into the producer who has a policeman as a guest on the set. It is common

Truffaut confronted by a Germanic challenge over the lack of both politics and eroticism in his films

practice to massage the local authorities when shooting a film. Certainly Nice is no exception.

As the set quietens down for a rehearsal, we are initially amused by Séverine's problem in remembering her lines, especially when she proposes saying numbers instead and demonstrates beautifully how she does it for 'Federico'. Valentina Cortesa had actually played a character called Valentina in Federico Fellini's 1965 film *Giulietta degli spiriti* (*Juliet of the Spirits*).

The Italian practice of not using the synchronous recording of dialogue is here affectionately lampooned. The bravura visual style of the best of Italian cinema owes much to the lack of concern for a good sound recording, since the camera can be used with complete freedom. Truffaut himself was in favour of dialogue replacement since he found it gave the opportunity to rewrite the dialogue one last time and to discover nuances in performance.

Our amusement at Séverine's difficulties turns to relief when the solution of writing the lines on sheets of paper and placing them at strategic points around the set seems likely to work. At this point the transformation of Odile from make-up girl into maid is destined to be the straw that breaks Séverine.

Séverine in distress, unable to deal with lines she can't remember and doors she can't distinguish

When the set is cleared Ferrand tells Alphonse he does not have to leave, but Alphonse decides to go to the cinema, which we have now been made to feel is preferable to watching the pain of cinema being made.

The way in which Valentina Cortesa sustains our belief in her problem with the door is acting of the highest order. Truffaut never has to cut at the decisive moment each time she mistakes the door because she is so convincing within the shot.

The vertical wipe of the frame at the end is very effective; holding for a moment on Alexandre and Séverine before concluding as the music supports the mood.

The problems and tensions of this scene are the natural precursor to Ferrand's nightmare as, for the first time, we see the boy walking down a side street. The black-and-white photography and the Expressionist images remind us of classic movies of the 30s.

If the Séverine crisis scene is wonderfully effective cinema then Stacey's reluctance to swim is just as ineffective. It seems to have been badly shot and perversely put together. Although we are in no doubt that tension is mounting, the edginess in this scene comes from an unusually ugly angle on most of the action. It is totally incomprehensible that Joëlle is seen trying to persuade Stacey to co-operate *before* Ferrand has asked her to intervene. Consequently, when she goes off to talk to her later, we cut to Stacey miraculously already in the pool. The odd thing is that this jigsaw actually fits together perfectly if assembled according to the script.

Fortunately, Truffaut is back on form in the next scene in the production office where Ferrand and Bertrand attempt to face up to the problem posed by Stacey's pregnancy. It is shot in one master shot, which is only interrupted once to allow us to identify the film books that arrive in a parcel for Ferrand.

In the script the problem of Stacey was supposed to have been added to by a law suit from the writer of the novel 'Je vous présente Paméla', reflecting the difficulty Truffaut had in real life with the claim to the title of *La Nuit américaine*.

It was certainly a felicitous idea at the end of this scene to use Delerue's music over a roll-call of Truffaut's best-loved directors: Dreyer, Lubitsch, Bergman, Godard, Hitchcock, Rossellini, Hawks, Bresson, Buñuel and Visconti. It is ironic that he should include Jean-Luc

Godard in this tribute considering Godard's response to the film and their subsequent rupture. On the other hand it is surprising that Renoir is missing.

We are helped in the transition to the airport by Delerue's music and the flash-frames inserted in the pan around the room before the cut to the taxiing airplane. The fractured rhythm is sustained by the seven cuts as Jacqueline Bisset as Julie is ushered through the crowd. Then there is a cut to the press conference, which thrusts us immediately and very effectively into the question session.

The arrival of Julie is elided with the arrival of 'Paméla'. Indeed there is no moment of meeting between the director and his star. Considering that Ferrand admits later to her husband that he has never before cast a leading lady without meeting her, and that this was true in reality as well, I think Truffaut deprived us of an important and poignant moment.

The flow from the arrival of the young couple to the gathering on the balcony is helped by inserts of camera mechanisms. Truffaut gives particular prominence to Jacqueline Bisset. She has the occasional close-up and a moment of voice-over, which is the only time a character apart from the director speaks to us in this way. It achieves a subjectivity which could have been used elsewhere in the film, especially in the episode when she sleeps with Alphonse.

When Ferrand and Alexandre meet Doctor Nelson at the bottom of the steps Doctor Nelson's speech is cut short by an inter-cut close-up of Jacqueline Bisset taking off her wig and turning to look past the camera as if someone has called her. There is a sort of magic about the way this evokes her presence. Yann Dedet extends the magic by cutting from her to a familiar crew member passing in front of the camera in close-up, smiling while eating an apple, which then reveals Julie as she comes down the steps to meet her husband. She pulls him away for a kiss. From the airport to this moment Truffaut has taken every opportunity to emphasise the star quality of his leading actress.

The start of the next scene is one of the best examples in the film of Truffaut's skill and economy with the camera. We track behind Ferrand as he approaches the stairs to the cutting room. He greets Stacey and they climb up together. As they enter the cutting room and he greets Yann and Martine the camera has craned up and zoomed in to a tight four-shot as they view the material. Only then do we cut: to the editing machine as Alexandre calls 'Stacey', and we are instantly drawn in to the sequence.

The façade of the lovers' bungalow leads us into the second set-piece of the film: the recalcitrant cat. The edgy exchange between Liliane and Alphonse is a lovely way of setting up the plot of this scene. Their intimacy is a crude imitation of the furtive couple's tryst.

Doctor Nelson appears and is given a seat by Ferrand. The doctor exchanges looks with his wife. The shot of Julie is actually a two-shot with Alexandre, but it has been optically matted with a 'flag' (a device used to control the beam of a light), so as to emphasise the intimacy between the two. The audacity of Truffaut is not so much that he enjoys using such a device but that two shots later the shot is used without the matte.

Throughout this scene the ability to 'mistreat the film, to knock it about' as Truffaut described it, is an object lesson to those whose slavish adherence to continuity makes for hackneyed films. Even more than in the Séverine 'cupboard' scene, the editing here creates another form of continuity, one which is more psychological than physical.

Somehow we reach take thirteen with the original cat. When Ferrand says 'get me a cat who can act' we have three short cuts on Joëlle

58   Manipulating the image: Truffaut mattes out Alexandre to isolate Julie in the shot

and Bernard, and her quick return with the studio cat is helped by Ferrand's voice-over: 'where is Joëlle?'

Yet when it comes to the triumphant take it is held from beginning to end in one shot, from the moment Bernard puts the cat down, to the exultant response of the crew after Ferrand finally says cut, save for an insert of Julie and Alexandre watching, after the cat has started to lap. The continuous action was imperative since, as Truffaut's mentor André Bazin said, 'When two or more elements are essential to a scene, cutting is forbidden.' Would we have believed the action if at the critical moment, as the cat is about to lap the milk, we had cut to another angle?

The conversation in the car between Doctor Nelson and Alexandre about the vulnerability of actors is supported by Delerue's most lyrical music, which at the same time conveys pathos. The reaction of Doctor Nelson on finding his present from Julie underlines the need for performers to feel loved. This is a scene which Claude Lelouch would have been proud of.

At the airport after Alexandre and Doctor Nelson have separated, there are three brief freeze frames, two on Alexandre and one on him and Christian after they have met. Truffaut's intention seems to be to hold the moment of this important rendezvous. They feel ominously like frames stolen by paparazzi.

Back at the studio, Ferrand is told that the kitchen scene must be shot tomorrow and Joëlle immediately accedes to working on the dialogue that night, as Suzanne Schiffman must have done on many similar occasions.

Shots of the hotel staircase and corridor act as a bridge to Ferrand's room where he is seen working on the script with Joëlle. Incorporating material such as this shows the desire to add punctuation between scenes. In this instance Truffaut and Yann Dedet achieve a sense of the sleeping hotel, in contrast to the director and his collaborator who are burning the midnight oil.

Ferrand is angry at the start of this scene because an American film, *The Godfather*, is dominating the cinemas in Nice. Despite his love of Hollywood, Truffaut was a champion of indigenous cinema. The craft in the writing, as this remark is linked to godsons by Joëlle, and then through *Lolita* to *Lorenzaccio*, is to be admired.

It is surprising that the reference to Alfred de Musset's play *Lorenzaccio* survived. In the play Alexander de Medici is killed by his younger cousin, Lorenzaccio. Thus the subsequent tragedy is subtly foretold. This allusion would be lost on anyone not familiar with nineteenth-century French drama. It is not what one would expect from a director concerned to hold an audience.

What is very authentic is the impression in this scene of how Truffaut worked on dialogue during this shoot and others, especially with Suzanne Schiffman. In this respect Nathalie Baye is very convincing as his collaborator.

The *mise en scène* is both simple and apposite. Joëlle sits throughout while the restless Ferrand dodges back and forth, now reading the paper, now moving the room service tray, now consulting the treatment pinned to the wall; all the while taking his time to settle to the task in hand until she takes the initiative and tells him to dictate while she types.

Ferrand makes the point that Julie, because of her Hollywood background, is the only one to understand the script. This belies the fact that both Alexandre and Séverine have spent much of their careers in Hollywood. I think Truffaut believed that the Americans understood narrative cinema better than anyone else, especially melodrama.

The telephone call which announces that a woman has called by for Ferrand is an effective device for getting us out of the room and down to the lobby, but it raises questions that are left unanswered in the film: why has the woman turned up? Is this a regular arrangement? Was Truffaut trying to pre-empt any criticism that his character stood aloof from the activity indulged in by the rest of the cast and crew?

Our curiosity is mirrored by that of Jean-François and Bernard, who observe the woman in the lobby. Their conjecture concludes with a reference to *Le Repos du guerrir* (1962) – 'Warrior's rest'. This was a film based on a novel of the same name made by Roger Vadim and starring Brigitte Bardot as a woman who gives comfort to an exhausted 'warrior'. Jean-François and Bernard then provide a link to the tribute to Jeanne Moreau, Truffaut's old friend, in the film quiz they watch on television.

Confirmation that the new dialogue has been completed comes as Julie's lines are slipped under her bedroom door and, as she starts to learn them, music takes us into the preparation for the kitchen scene. Truffaut's somewhat peremptory instructions to the actors are apparently a fair reflection of his approach; trusting that his casting was effective.

The frenetic activity of the crew contrasts with the calm among the actors. Despite it being a night shoot Christian is on hand to watch his 'godfather'. Symbolically he takes the seat vacated by the older man.

I am intrigued by the subsequent altercation between Truffaut and Jean-Pierre Léaud. I use their real names since this apparently reflects the truth of their less than smooth relationship during the shoot. Yet both seem happy to imitate their relationship on screen.

In the elaborate montage to music there are many moments of direction, acting and craft work which are presented in brief cameos, while Delerue's triumphant music celebrates the medium. The interest is in two kinds of image. The first are those stolen from scenes that did not make the final cut and the second are casual moments, as it were, off camera.

In the first category is the effect on the face of Alexandre achieved by the movement of a flag in front of a lamp, to imitate the door closing as Séverine leaves the room (the solution to her problem in finding the right door that was not used at the time).

The second group of images include those of Valentina Cortesa and Jacqueline Bisset as they view some contact prints. Even here Yann Dedet has inserted a quick shot of their legs. The shot of Cortesa taking

Montage of the film-making process

off her wig and laughing is perhaps the most memorable of all. There follows an inexplicable shot of a huge statue of Abraham Lincoln as it is wheeled across the back-lot. It is difficult to comprehend the significance of this image; unless Truffaut is implying that the American juggernaut rides roughshod over European cinema!

The subsequent cocktail party, a relatively simple scene of one-and-a-half minutes based on two master shots, contains eighteen cuts. The statue of Lincoln appears again behind the children playing cards, which is used as a buffer between the two halves of the scene; that is between the discussion of Alexandre's plan to adopt Christian and the introduction of the stuntman.

Delerue's *bal musette* music continues throughout as Yann Dedet makes a series of unforced cuts simply to keep the scene flowing. No concern is shown for literal continuity as characters jump from shot to shot, functioning as threads in the editor's intricate pattern.

We fade out on the laughing group of Ferrand, Julie and the stuntman. They are laughing because 'Truffaut' says he speaks English very well but doesn't understand it! This is in response to the question of whether he will ever make a film in England. Indeed, Truffaut is joking about an experience which was less than comfortable for him when making *Fahrenheit 451* (see Postscript).

As Liliane joins the crew leaving for the location shoot, Delerue's music takes on a Western feel, the cue coming from Jean-François' exhortation: 'To horse!'

The mood of the casual lovemaking between Bernard and Joëlle on the river bank is continued in the ripe badinage at the stunt site. It is as if being on location has released the crew from constraints that they felt at the studio. When Joëlle arrives with Bernard, Liliane is quick to notice that she has swapped her white blouse for a striped sweater. Her reference to a lack of continuity is particularly apt.

Liliane's departure with the stuntman is swift and surprising, especially because until the film has come back from the laboratory the following day there is no certainty that the shoot has worked satisfactory, however confident the camera operators are. He may still be required for re-shoots. Plot, it seems, overrides logic on this occasion.

Back at the studios Liliane's remark to Julie that she doesn't see why everyone should suffer because of Alphonse's unhappy childhood is a poignant reminder of the background shared by Léaud and Truffaut.

Stacey arrives unbelievably pregnant in time to join the group photo. The section where Julie tells Alphonse about Liliane's departure is supported by Delerue's agitated score, which allows us to watch their conversation without hearing what is said. The cutting makes us aware that Pierre seems to be gloating and that Madame Lajoie is storing up this latest scandal for her subsequent diatribe.

It is here that Joëlle makes her classic remark that she could leave a bloke for a film but never a film for a bloke. Nathalie Baye remembered that it took her an embarrassing number of takes to get the phrase the right way round, since she found the remark unbelievable.

The music that concludes the nightmare as the stills from *Citizen Kane* are stolen is cathartic in its resolution, which suggests that the successful steal is satisfying to the dreamer. That a boy so young would find stills from such a film desirable must have seemed incomprehensible to the majority of the audience in 1973. Even Truffaut's predilection at that age might well have been for pin-ups of the latest female star rather than a serious movie.

The strange image that follows of Jacqueline Bisset climbing a ladder in her bare feet and with her dress partially tucked into her

Julie/Pamela greets her in-laws from the false window

knickers would certainly have fitted the bill of a pin-up image. Since there is no explanation of why the young couple are staying across the road from the villa the image was obviously too important to Truffaut to warrant logic.

This scene recalls an occasion during the shooting of *Les Deux anglaises et le continent* when the young man, played by Jean-Pierre Léaud, looks out of his bedroom window across to the house of the two sisters. A false window had to be made for this scene as no house existed within view of the other.

The visual deceit of the false window is added to by the adjustment of the scene to cover the absence of Alphonse. There is also another cover-up here: when one looks closely one can see that Walter Bal, the camera operator, is wearing a heavy poncho, despite the fact that everyone else is dressed in light clothing. This was to hide the bandages from a motorcycle accident that he and Pierre-William Glenn had had *en route* to a party given by Valentina Cortesa at a country restaurant on the Corniche. Glenn signed himself out of the hospital against medical advice less than twenty-four hours after the accident, because he was determined to avoid being replaced on the picture.

Odile and Bernard are startled by ...

The scene in which Joëlle mounts the stairs in the hotel and, without her glasses, mistakes the door and surprises Odile in bed with Bernard, includes one of the most delightful cuts in the film. The shock of one woman discovered by the other is mirrored in the two faces. Then Joëlle breaks into a smile and mouths an apology.

At her farewell meal Séverine runs the gamut of emotions from elation to melancholy in a brief moment. Provoked by some production stills, she bemoans the fact that the work of cinema is transitory. Valentina Cortesa holds us in thrall just as she holds her colleagues. It is ironic that this woman of theatre, where performance only remains alive in the minds of the audience, should remark on the ephemeral nature of cinema.

As they mount the stairs, Alexandre recounts a story about Séverine, whose reputation was so high in her native Italy that a director they had worked for together had kept insisting that she was better than the great Eleanora Duse. He had dubbed her, Alexandre says, 'Duse-et-demi' (twelve-and-a-half), a reference to Fellini's *Otto e mezzo* (*8½*).

This story is an appropriate precursor to a Felliniesque moment when Alphonse appears in the corridor, wraith-like in a long white nightshirt, and asks if anyone will lend him the money to go to a brothel.

... an amused Joëlle

Ferrand's speech as he leads Alphonse back to his room, about films being more harmonious than life such that people who work in film are often people who are only truly happy when they are working reflects Truffaut's own feelings. His pell-mell delivery, however, makes the words seem more learnt than felt. It is perhaps significant that the whole speech is played on Alphonse, since his compliance seems more by hypnotism than conviction. However, he is obviously immune to Ferrand's appeal to his sense of dedication. Later when Julie pleads for him to stay he claims that he has believed women to be magical for too long.

Alphonse's survey has been a continuing motif from early on in the film, as have the images of Madame Lajoie and of the gates of the studios. Truffaut was very fond of repetition as a device. Cinema is a linear medium. This encourages and supports the driving narrative which is an inherent part of conventional films. However, if the film-maker wishes to make the audience reflect, then it is essential to offer elements that echo each other, so that the viewer is reminded of earlier moments and made to think in other, more non-linear ways.

The lighting for the scene between Julie and Alphonse is very disappointing: it is clinical with no atmosphere. Considering it is supposed to be night it would have been better under-lit than over. Is this an oversight or is it meant to emphasise that there is no real feeling between the two?

Joëlle concludes that everyone on the film is crazy and confirms that her dedication is of the kind all films need and most film crews somehow manage to acquire, regardless of the project's worth – which is, after all, Truffaut's point.

Truffaut films Julie leaving Alphonse the next morning in one shot while Delerue's music reinforces the mood of regret and anxiety. Director, editor and composer have contrived to choreograph the scene so that every slight movement of Julie as she wakes and confronts the day is matched by a new sustained chord.

Alphonse makes his fateful call to Doctor Nelson. Truffaut remarked that he would not have asked any other actor to perform this piece:

> That's a scene I would certainly not write for an actor I didn't know, but it goes so well with the idea of Jean-Pierre Léaud, with what one has seen him do in other films, with what he's like a little in life too,

that the scene simply forced itself on me and no sooner had the idea struck me than I found it highly amusing and wrote it. [34]

The writing and Truffaut's *mise en scène* allow the drama in the production office over Alphonse and Julie to evolve organically. The in-depth staging of the scene is reminiscent of the Renoir of *Le Crime de Monsieur Lange*.

It is the urbane Alexandre whose comments, from the point-of-view of someone who has seen it all before, make us conscious that the incipient farce/melodrama should be kept in perspective. This is after all not a Greek tragedy, despite his reference to the House of Atreus.

Outside Julie's room it is Joëlle that puts two and two together when Lajoie appears and confirms that Alphonse can't be found. Lajoie, as always, is accompanied by his wife who, having remained the silent observer up until now, suddenly releases a diatribe against cinema, or more precisely the people who make films. Madame Lajoie has been an ever present figure during the shoot. She can be spotted in the background of almost every scene; even during the one with the recalcitrant cat. (I regret her absence from the stunt location where the badinage would have further fuelled her invective.)

It is common, as Ferrand implies when commenting on the policeman who visits the set, to feel when making a film that the guillotine is about to fall or the trapdoor is about to open as the rope tightens around your neck, and that observers are hoping to be there when it happens. In sharing Renoir's belief that films should be made with joy, it is almost as if Truffaut felt guilty and each time he experienced that special pleasure he was tempting fate. In this case it is the attendant pleasure taken in physical relationships among the cast and crew that Madame Lajoie objects to the most.

Truffaut once said that in all his films the activity of the crew and cast off the set reflected an important aspect of the particular script he was shooting. For instance, on *Jules et Jim* everyone played dominoes and on *Fahrenheit 451* everybody was an avid reader of books. Can we assume that *La Nuit américaine* was a joyful experience in its own way?

There are many cuts in Madame Lajoie's speech, most of which are not necessary, but they give an edginess to the scene without calling attention to themselves, mainly because of Yann Dedet's immaculate control of rhythm. A lesser editor would have made considerable use of reaction shots, but Dedet stays on her face throughout.

As Ferrand delivers the butter to Julie, Dedet makes a pointed cut to emphasise a Jean Cocteau motif on a small tapestry on the wall. What did Truffaut want the observant spectator to pick up by this reference to Cocteau? He is remembered for a handful of films – including *Le Sang d'un poète* (1930), *La Belle et la bête* (1996), *Orphée* (1950), and *Le Testament d'Orphée* (1959) – but he did not consider that film-making was his profession. Rather, he considered himself a poet who occasionally made films, bringing a poet's sensibility to the cinema.

Although Truffaut admired this kind of cinema, he was conscious of his own need to please his audience with films that were first and foremost entertainment. However he certainly identified with something Cocteau once said in an interview:

> in France, film making is a family affair, and no-one rebels if his prerogatives are encroached upon – lighting, sets, costumes, make-up, music and so forth. All this rests in my hands and I work in close collaboration with my assistants. Consequently, as my unit itself

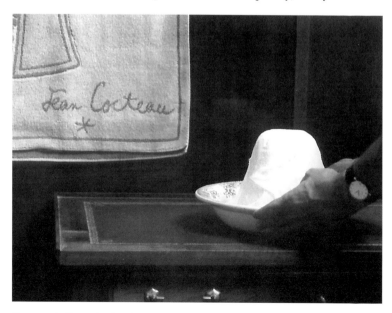

70   The mound of butter is placed deliberately beside the Cocteau motif

admits, the film becomes a thing of my very own to which they have contributed by their advice and skill.[35]

This statement by Cocteau predates the 'auteur' theory by a number of years. It is also in many ways close to Truffaut's own attitude, which was less dogmatic and autocratic than that espoused by the more belligerent members of the *nouvelle vague*.

Cocteau adopted a young man in much the same way that Alexandre wants to adopt Christian. Indeed, Edouard Dermit became heir to Cocteau's estate. Truffaut acknowledged this connection and would have appreciated the value of being 'adopted' since his own life was transformed when André Bazin took him into his home and treated him as one of the family. After Bazin's death Truffaut did all he could to support his widow, Janine, as if it was his duty as her 'son'.

I have no idea what connection, if any, Truffaut wants us to make between the Cocteau reference and the crucial scene with Julie. Although Jacqueline Bisset gives a convincing portrayal of her distress and shame it's disappointing that Truffaut did not shoot the scene with his usual élan. A developing two-shot would have been more effective, but perhaps he was too self-conscious of his own performance to want to intrude into the frame during Bisset's big moment. I am reminded of those beautiful stills of Truffaut and Jeanne Moreau when they were making *Jules et Jim*. They are sitting on a bench talking and laughing together, and it would have been marvellous if he had been able to animate a similar moment between himself and one of the women in this film.

This is the man who was quoted as saying, 'tristesse sans fin, sont les films sans femmes' (sadness without end are films without women) and who reflected that for him the natural process of making a film was that for the period of each shoot his close relationship with his female star on set was mirrored by a similar closeness off set.

The truth is, one feels, that Truffaut created the scene between himself and Bisset mainly to illustrate Ferrand's laser-like focus on the film itself, and that despite the circumstances, the words uttered by Julie in her traumatic state are useful fodder for his own script.

His single-minded preoccupation is revealed when, in the scene in which the anxious Alphonse is being made up, the camera pans to discover Ferrand who is quietly finishing the new lines for Julie which he gives to Odile to take to her dressing room.

As Julie receives her new lines, we see not only Doctor Nelson in the mirror, but the microphone boom, an unusual example of the technology intruding in a scene not from the film within the film. Even if it is a mistake this almost passes as a subtle attempt to remind us that all is artifice.

The shoot of the 'false candle' scene proceeds with a quiet professionalism, born of the consciousness of all present of the delicate situation between Alphonse and Julie. 'Acting' is frequently under pressure of this kind. Ferrand has decided to use music as playback in the scene; which is not necessary but which relates to the era of silent cinema when musicians would play on the set to create the appropriate mood.

I think Truffaut had a second purpose, for when the shooting is interrupted by the announcement of the death of Alexandre the music has created the right atmosphere for the shocked reaction. Appropriate shots of those most affected by the news are inserted with two exceptions: first, Julie is not seen, and second, the shot of Ferrand is snatched and awkward.

It is a film-maker's biggest fear that a cast member might die during a shoot. Nathalie Baye told me that this had happened on a subsequent film she had worked on. She also said that each new project she is involved in, something happens to connect it to an incident in *La*

Nuit américaine. It was Françoise Dorleac, Truffaut's close friend and star of *Le Peau douce*, who in 1967 tragically burned to death when her car overturned on the way to the airport in Nice. Truffaut had planned to make a documentary on the woman he called affectionately 'Framboise'. This moment in *La Nuit américaine* shows Truffaut again using real life events for his script. Ironically it was with Dorleac's sister, Catherine Deneuve, that Truffaut subsequently had one of his most intense and affecting relationships.

There is no logic to the shot of Ferrand driving around the desolate exterior set as he ponders the death of Alexandre and it was not in the script. Jean-François Stevenin remembers this shot being invented by Truffaut and he considers it to be one of the most beautiful in the film. It happened that an actor was not made up in time and without knowing for what purpose, this shot was set up and taken at nine o'clock in the morning in the rain. It provides the background for Truffaut's/Ferrand's most direct statement:

> Along with Alexandre, a whole era of moviemaking is fast disappearing. Films will soon be shot in the streets – without stars,

Ferrand drives around the desolate exterior set as he contemplates the completion of the film after the death of Alexandre

without scripts. A production like 'Je vous présente Paméla' will soon be obsolete.

It is true that the Victorine Studio itself saw no feature shooting on its stages for many years, but this sounds more like the battle cry of the New Wave a dozen years earlier than the way cinema was moving in the 70s.

The artifice of film is once again asserted as we see the projector before we watch the last rushes of Alexandre which conclude with his clowning gesture of climbing the balustrade, while Séverine restrains him. We are reminded of Alphonse's childishness as Julie has to act in his absence at the window.

We then have the discussion with the insurers, played by Marcel Berbert and Graham Greene, about the completion of the film. Considering the production executive's and novelist's lack of experience in front of the camera Truffaut was audacious in shooting the whole scene in one developing shot; with the movements of the camera and the characters substituting for cutting. The suggestion of shooting the death of the double in the snow – actually made by Suzanne Schiffman – reminds us of that beautiful moment of the death of Marie Dubois in *Tirez sur le pianiste*.

Truffaut is confronted by insurance imperatives conveyed by Graham Greene

The snow is prepared and Ferrand expresses his concern that it not be too white. Bernard reassures him with a movie buff's reference to *La Neige était sale* (*The Snow was Dirty*), a French thriller made in 1952.

Alphonse has had an offer to make a film in Tokyo. It is *First Love* by Turgenev. (A version of this was made in 1970 with, coincidentally, Valentina Cortesa in a lead role.)

The shoot begins and, as Alphonse runs off, the music starts and we go into a montage with many cuts before we hear Ferrand say: 'merci toute le monde!' The image fades out on our familiar crew. The fact that the film within the film has come full circle, at least in shooting terms, is very neat, even though there is no attempt to explain why on one occasion Alphonse chases Alexandre to slap his face and at another time, but in the same place, he shoots him.

The next day everyone is leaving including the editing team, Yann and Martine, who will finish their job in Paris. The shot is a little reminder of that famous image from the birth of cinema, the Lumière brothers', *Workers Leaving a Factory*.

Bernard is thrust into the spotlight by volunteering to speak to the television crew about the progress of the film. His insistence that it went perfectly is absolutely sincere. His challenge to the lens and therefore to the audience that he hopes the public will enjoy watching the film as much as they have enjoyed making it, could almost be a Shakespearean ending, reminiscent of *A Midsummer Night's Dream*. This analogy is not entirely irrelevant considering both the machinations of the characters and the participation of the 'mechanicals' in Shakespeare's play; a motley crew who are treated with considerable affection by the playwright, just as Truffaut reveals his love for his own crew.

The end titles with Delerue's Vivaldi-like theme celebrate the actors, and therefore both cast and crew, who each have their vignettes. How wonderful it would be to also see the other crew members who do not appear in front of the camera: from Suzanne Schiffman to Pierre-William Glenn to Georges Delerue.

The last shot from the helicopter places the Victorine Studios in the context of its surroundings; in a final confirmation of the prosaic environment of this 'dream factory'. *La Nuit américaine* becomes just another episode in the process of creating the fragile façade that is cinema.

POSTSCRIPT

....

Some time after the release of *La Nuit américaine*, Truffaut decided to publish the post-production script coupled with the diary he had while shooting *Fahrenheit 451* in England in 1966. The first entry in that diary bears an uncanny similarity to the script of *La Nuit américaine*. Truffaut reports the fact that Julie Christie failed the insurance medical because of her exhaustion after nine months on *Doctor Zhivago*. The start of the shoot had to be delayed. It was a bad augury.

However well prepared a film-maker may feel he/she is for a shoot, it is still in the lap of the gods whether the elements will come together in a positive and creative fashion. In the case of *Fahrenheit 451* Truffaut had waited three-and-a-half years to bring this Ray Bradbury story to the screen. Coincidentally, Artists Associés had refused to back the project just as they later turned down *La Nuit américaine*. At no point had he envisaged it to be shot in England, having explored many options around the world from Stockholm to Brasília.

While he had no quarrel with the skilful and charming crew, led by Nic Roeg on camera, and he immediately fell in love with Julie Christie, he had a difficult time with Oscar Werner who, according to Truffaut's own account, since their time working together on *Jules et Jim*, had acquired an ego to match his star status. Just as disturbingly, Truffaut knew he did not have a grasp of the nuances of the language, and was not confident of his ability to direct performances in English effectively. Perhaps most importantly, and despite the presence of Suzanne Schiffman, he missed his 'film family'. The size of the crew he commented, 'would make Jean Vigo turn in his grave'.

It is therefore disarming of Truffaut to put this frank and often disturbing story alongside his script of the film that celebrates cinema. Perhaps he felt he had missed a dimension of the life in film. Or perhaps he was sensitive to the fact that by association his critics bracketed him with Ferrand and the world of melodramatic cinema portrayed in 'Je vous présente Paméla'.

We should not underestimate the intelligence of Truffaut's cinema. Although he had little conventional education his development as a critic under the eyes of André Bazin gave him as good a grasp of film as his fellow comrades, Godard, Rohmer, Chabrol and Rivette. In my opinion he was the most instinctive film-maker of them all. If his films were more commercial and successful than his colleagues, then this is a measure of their consummate craftmanship as well as their wide appeal.

Probably no director in the history of cinema has started his career with three such effective and affecting films as *Les Quatre cents coups*, *Tirez sur le pianiste*, and *Jules et Jim*. That he subsequently failed to retain such a high consistentcy is not surprising. No director ever can. In the end *La Nuit américaine* should be seen simply for what it is: a celebration of the medium to which François Truffaut made a unique and unforgettable contribution.

In his foreword to the collection of Truffaut's letters, Jean-Luc Godard wrote: 'François est peut-être mort. Je suis peut-être vivant. Il n'y a pas de difference, n'est-ce pas' (François is perhaps dead. I am perhaps alive. There is no difference, is there)?

NOTES

. . . .

1 François Truffaut, *Les Films de ma vie* (Paris: Flammarion, 1975), p. 14.
2 Ibid., p. 253.
3 Gilles Jacob and Claude de Givray (eds), *François Truffaut: Correspondance* (Paris: Hatier, 1998), p. 479.
4 Ibid., p. 480.
5 Ibid., p. 485.
6 *Le Roman de François Truffaut* (Paris: Cahiers du cinéma/Editions de l'Etoile, 1985), p. 68.
7 Ibid., p. 72
8 François Truffaut, with Jean-Louis Richard and Suzanne Schiffman, *La Nuit américane, scenario du film* (Paris: Cinéma 2000/Editions Seghers, 1974), p. 5.
9 Ibid., p. xx.
10 Ibid., p. xx.
11 Ibid., p. xx.
12 Ibid., p. xx.
13 Ibid., p. xx.
14 *Le Roman de François Truffaut*, p. 89.
15 Anne Gilian (ed.), *Le Cinéma selon François Truffaut* (Paris: Flammarion, 1988), p. 306.
16 Damien Lanfranchi, letter to the author.

17 *François Truffaut: Correspondance*, p. 467.
18 Jacqueline Bisset, interview with the author.
19 Ibid.
20 Nathalie Baye, interview with the author.
21 Nike Arrighi-Borghese, letter to the author.
22 Interview in *Jeune Cinéma*, no. 77, March 1974.
23 Ibid.
24 Lanfranchi, letter to the author.
25 Interview in *Téléciné*, no. 94, March 1961.
26 *Le Roman de François Truffaut*, p. 99.
27 Yann Dedet, interview with the author.
28 *Cinéma et Télécinéma*, no. 341, October 1966.
29 *Jeune Cinéma*, no. 77, March 1974.
30 Ibid.
31 *Le Roman de François Truffaut*, p. 138.
32 *Les Films de ma vie*.
33 Jean Narboni and Serge Toubiana (eds), *Le Plaisir des yeux* (Paris: Flammarion, 1987).
34 *Jeune Cinéma*, no. 77, March 1974.
35 *Cocteau on the Film* (conversations with André Fraigneau; New York: Dover, 1972), p. 72.

CREDITS

· ·

La Nuit américaine

France/Italy
1973
**Cannes film festival
screening**
14 May 1973
**French commercial
release**
24 May 1973
Production companies
Les Films du Carrosse (Paris)
P.E.C.F. (Paris)
P.I.C. (Rome)
Director
François Truffaut
Screenplay
François Truffaut
Jean-Louis Richard
Suzanne Schiffman
Director of photography
Pierre-William Glenn
Camera operator
Walter Bal
Assistant cameramen
Dominique Chapuis
Jean-François Gondre
Chief electrician
Jean-Claude Gasche
Art director
Damien Lanfranchi
Costumes
Monique Dury
Make-up
Fernande Hugi
Thi Loan N'Guyen
Hair
Malou Rossignol
Set photographer
Pierre Zucca
Assistant directors
Suzanne Schiffman
Jean-François Stevenin
Script-girl
Christine Pellé
Film editors
Yann Dedet
Martine Barraqué
Sound
René Levert
Boom operator
Harrick Maury

Dubbing mixer
Antoine Bonfanti
Music
Georges Delerue
Production administrator
Christian Lentretien
Production manager
Claude Miller
Executive producer
Marcel Berbert
Unit production manager
Roland Thenot
**Assistant to unit
production manager**
Alex Maineri

The actors who play actors:
Jacqueline Bisset
Julie Baker/Paméla
Valentina Cortese
Séverine
Alexandra Stewart
Stacey
Jean-Pierre Aumont
Alexandre
Jean-Pierre Léaud
Alphonse
The actors who play
technicians:
François Truffaut
Ferrand, the director
Jean Champion
Bertrand, the producer
Nathalie Baye
Joëlle, the script-girl
Dani
Liliane, her apprentice
Bernard Menez
Bernard, the props man
Nike Arrighi
Odile, the make-up girl
Gaston Joly
Lajoie, production manager
The others:
Maurice Seveno
The television reporter
David Markham
Doctor Nelson
Zénaide Rossi
Madame Lajoie

Christophe Vesque
The boy with the cane
Mark Boyle
The stuntman
Xavier Saint-Macary
Christian, the young man
Marcel Berbert
French insurance broker
**'Henry Graham'
(Graham Greene)**
English insurance broker
Note: Several technicians
appeared in the film playing
themselves including:
Jean-François Stévenin,
Pierre Zucca, Damien
Lanfranchi, Walter Bal,
Yann Dedet and Martine
Barraqué.

116 minutes
10,437 feet

**Eastmancolor, Spherical
Panavision**

Filmed at the Victorine
Studios, Nice and on
location on the Cote d'Azur
from late September to
December 1972.

1973 Academy Award for
Best Foreign Film.
1973 National Society of
Film Critics and the New
York Critics' Circle awards:
Best Picture, Best Director,
Best Supporting Actress
(Valentina Cortese).

The print of *La Nuit
américaine* in the National
Film and Television Archive
was aquired specially for the
360 Classic Feature Films
project from Warner Bros.
Distributors.

ALSO PUBLISHED

. . . .

If you would like further information about future BFI Film Classics or about other books on film, media and popular culture from BFI Publishing, please write to:

BFI Film Classics
BFI Publishing
21 Stephen Street
London W1P 2LN